Blessings ♡
Loylene

Keep Turning

Turning Toward the Sun (7 Ways My Mom Inspires Me to Live Without Her)

Published by: Denesha Chambers, In partnership with YBF Publishing LLC.

www.deneshachambers.com

Manufactured in the United States of America

Cover Design by: Angela Kelly of Inked Pixels Company

Edited By: Nia Sadé Akinyemi, The Literary Revolutionary. www.theliteraryrevolutionary.com

ISBN #: 978-0-9968910-4-2

Follow Author Denesha Chambers

Facebook.com/AuthorDeneshaChambers

Instagram/Twitter: @AuthorDChambers

www.deneshachambers.com

Turning Toward The Sun

7 Ways My Mom Inspires Me to Live Without Her

Denesha Chambers

Table of Contents

Dedicated to Ma

I am, because you were... loving, strong, and faithful. Perhaps with a side of crazy but, you always poured and spoke life into me. Now you live on in my heart, dreams, and these pages. A thousand times a thousand...

THANK YOU!

My mom, my angel.

Acknowledgments

Disclaimer: This is lengthy. What can I say, I'm thankful!

(See Chapter 5)

First and foremost, I would like to give honor and thanks to my Lord and savior Jesus Christ, who has perfectly orchestrated my life to date. Though I do not fully understand your ways sometimes, I believe they are all for my good. To my mother, Gail, thank you for your timeless love and life lessons. I love and miss you more than words can express. To my pops, James, a wonderful example of fatherhood, you've always been there to love and support me and for that I am truly grateful. I pray you go nowhere anytime soon. To my husband, Henry, thank you for listening, supporting, and sacrificing while I dreamt, and while I worked on birthing this book to existence. To my precious "baby boys", Henry III and Dean, your love and laughter have turned many tough days to better days. I'm lucky to be your mother. To my siblings, Teenya, Traci, and LaRon. I couldn't have adjusted the way I have without each of you. To Angela, Kim, Earl, Zdany, Shamika, Fawna, Linda, and Gloria, thank you for your enthusiastic and selfless willingness to share your love and loss experiences about your mothers. To Kalila, Danielle, Buky, and Claire, thank you for your encouraging words, inspiration, and feedback during this process. You are the iron that sharpens my iron. To Candace L. and Charnell, thank you for loving on me, but especially for filling in the gap when mom died. Last but not least, thank you to my literary coach and editor, Nia Sadé Akinyemi. Your encouragement, passion, and knowledge has been invaluable and contagious. Thank you!

Introduction

I wish someone had told me that losing my mother would be unlike any pain I've ever experienced. I wish I would have asked more questions when childhood friends met this unfortunate reality way too soon. I wish I'd known what the hell *pancreatic cancer* was before the doctors diagnosed my mom with this terminal illness. I wish I would have educated myself more on it when they did. I wish mom didn't have to go so soon.

These are just a few wishes out of the hundreds I have pondered in my process of bereavement since my mom, Ms. Gail Ernestine Bishop (Stewart) died on November 8, 2012 at 6:13a.m. In truth, I did not recognize the extent of how good I had it when she was still here. Don't get me wrong, we had a good relationship, but there is something about her absence that has brought about greater understanding and appreciation for her. Of course, when it comes to losing a mother, this is not always the case - I am not naive to that fact. Yet, in the case of Gail, whom I simply addressed as "*Ma*", nothing could be closer to the truth.

Ma is truly missed, hence, the purpose of this book. The presence of shock, confusion, anger, sadness, appreciation, etc. have all been a part of my journey since she passed. Each of them will be explored, including several others, to foster what grief and loss expert Alan Wolfelt termed as a "companioning" on this journey of being a member of the *mother loss* tribe.

Though losing my mother has been a very personal journey, this book won't be all personal. As a licensed therapist, I will share from my professional perspective as well, in hopes to promote greater insight into this human experience we call grief. The education on grief, bereavement, and mourning should be helpful for those of us that have difficulty being present with our stuff (i.e. feelings and pain). No judgment here. In some ways it is a survival tactic in order to keep breathing and stay above water, figuratively speaking. I know just how painful losing a mother can be, no matter the sort of relationship between the two of you and survival is one of our most primitive instincts as human beings.

Part of my approach in therapy is utilizing the narrative (stories) of clients to gain understanding that can facilitate a warm, yet productive means. This promotes positive outcomes such as an improvement in mood and/or better management of their problems. Therefore, consider this story, as one of the several I will share for your supportive needs:

If you knew her, you knew that Ma could talk, and talk, and talk with ease in normal circumstances. On occasion she would be requested to speak at local conferences to provide her own "experience, strength, and hope" in recovery. Even though she was a talkative person, she would very reluctantly accept these requests. Ma may have agreed to be the one to speak, and subsequently prepare what she was going to say, but for my siblings and me, her agreements were no walk in the park.

The upcoming months that led up to each event, we would have to hear her anxious rants about how much she did not want to follow through on the "commitment". Yet, as much as she complained she would keep each commitment, for she took any commitment she made very seriously. Ma let us know that she only complained because she did not believe she was a good speaker and she often was self-conscious about sounding bad to the dozens or hundreds of attendees who would be present for these conferences and workshops. It is worth mentioning that these sessions were recorded, which added to her already significant level of angst. Nonetheless, I can recall Ma relying on transparency, humor, and positive self talk to get her through these speaking "commitments". For example, at the onset of each workshop she would actually advise attendees that she hated to speak in front of large groups and didn't believe she was a good speaker at all.

Ma was quite wise, possibly unbeknownst to herself, especially since her delivery would often be stated in an abrupt manner. Let's just say she was your typical Yankee, born and raised in New York City. Nonetheless, I would credit her in this instance, for teaching me not to shy away from a challenge, but instead to acknowledge and address the negative feelings as my truth and push through. To her point, I profess to you, that I did not study Journalism or English in college. (Thank God for

Editors!) So, I humbly submit this text with my perspective as a counseling professional that knows firsthand the immense difficulties of becoming a part of the *mother loss* tribe. Pancreatic Cancer painstakingly qualified me as such on November 8th, 2012. Ever since it has been a journey of going from grief to mourning to being in hot pursuit of a greater purpose.

Please understand that in no way is this process linear, as implied. In fact, it is quite the contrary. Nonetheless, I have arrived to a place in the process that I hope will be of some encouragement to others that face this same major life change. In my healing process, many paths have led me to greater understanding about myself, my mom, and life in general. The reflection and introspection that has been a part of that process has led me to believe that my mom actually prepared me and my siblings both consciously and unconsciously to live this life even in her absence. The best way to illustrate this theory is in the sayings and life principles she often verbalized. I will share several examples of these throughout the book. These sayings and life principles were helpful while she was here and have just as much impact (or more) now that she is gone. Hence, you can expect that sharing them in company of my own personal experiences in an effort to promote others in and out the tribe, will do the same. For our personal experiences create a narrative/story, that holds our truth and our truth can be used as a vehicle that takes us on a journey to find what we need.

In the context of losing a mom, the need often will be comfort, peace, and healing. I encourage us all to be in hot pursuit of meeting those needs. In addition, to the account of my own personal experiences and stories, I have included professional insight to educate on the topic of grief and other relevant subject matter to death and loss. There's a saying that goes, "when you know better, you do better." Of course, I don't advocate a performance based approach to grief at all. Yet, it may be helpful to know more about these things called grief, mourning, and bereavement as a way to give yourself permission to be an active participant in the process without self-condemnation, but with compassion. Lastly, there are additional accounts of men and women who have lost their mothers towards the end of this book. They share their narratives that come from a variety of perspectives and circumstances to the loss of their mothers, and how they have been able to cope.

This is *Turning Toward the Sun's* purpose because the ultimate hope I believe Ma has for me is to be MBP (Motherless but Purposeful), despite the not so happy and fun moments of mother loss. While losing a mom can cast a shadow, and moments of distinct darkness, my hope is that you find a way to keep turning toward the sun. Figuratively, the "sun" is a place of warmth, comfort, peace, and maybe, most importantly, inspiration - to obtain the recharge necessary for the strength to readjust to a life forever changed by the loss of your mother. Ma tried to tell me the day would come when she would no longer be here. I did my best to ignore her but, once again, she was right and I don't like it AT ALL. Still,

I am thankful she also frequently told me she loved me, that she believed in me and that I would be used by God for good and great things. Nothing and nobody can ever take those things away from me, not even her death. She lives on in me. That has inspired me in ways I would not have imagined. You, too, can keep turning toward the sun in your loss situation. Remember, even during the worst storm, the sun will still rise and be there when the storm passes… and storms do eventually pass.

(1)

"Here's the thing..."

"Here's the thing..." Ma would always say that as a precursor to whatever nugget of wisdom, insight, or just plain ol' simple advice she was about to impart to whomever she was speaking to. It came to be quite comical really, because she almost always had wisdom, insight, or an opinion to offer. To her credit this was not out of pure egotism. She actually was a very observant (borderline *nosey*) person, possessing strong investigative skills, and was highly resourceful. Those three characteristics validated her insights and people would usually take heed.

As I've learned how to cope and continue on the journey of healing since she has been gone, I have utilized my own observation, investigative, and resourcefulness skills and abilities. Not quite to the same level as her, for there are levels to it, but let us just say to the extent

I'm able - it has been helpful. For example, although I was already a licensed therapist, I knew very little about grief and loss. Yet, since she has passed I have been exposed and greatly more aware of how prevalent loss and dying occurs. Of course, it has a little to do with the fact that I'm aging, as we all are. However, in truth, I am simply more aware of loss in my life, those that I know, and in the community at large. By losing my mother, I guess you can say my eyes have been opened.

Being the inquisitive person that I am, I went into pursuit of knowledge on grief and loss to show me "how to" grieve. While that was fairly naive of me at the time, by seeking that information I quickly learned the truths about it. Therefore, I was able to give myself certain permissions to take my own path on this bereavement journey and mourn in my own way. Through greater understanding of loss and with a heightened awareness of it around me, self-care and compassion toward myself and others grew. The compassion towards myself was comforting, and the self-care was healing and necessary. Both of these, I've desperately needed on countless occasions since November 8, 2012. Without taking some time educating myself more on grief and loss, through investigation, research and observations, in addition to using and obtaining resources, I cannot say I would have readily been able to adapt.

In true Gail-like fashion, allow me to share information and insights that might be helpful in a similar fashion. Let us take the power out the silence and get into this topic we have been thrown into.

Here's the thing.

Grief is an emotional response to a loss primarily processed internally. A loss can occur in any area of our lives: physical (a decline in health); financial (identity theft); occupational (job loss); social (divorce); mental (unmet expectations); and personal (death of a loved one). We will primarily focus on the grief of losing a loved one, specifically mothers, which is a process termed as bereavement. Nevertheless, these concepts can absolutely be applicable to any one of the other forms of loss.

When we grieve, we are having an internal relationship with our loss. We are processing our loss in a manner that is psychological, emotional, and mental. Hence, the roller coaster of emotional experiences. Oftentimes, persons seek out grief and bereavement counseling due to the uncomfortable nature of such swings in their moods and emotional state. They wonder if they are going "crazy." Those that don't seek help from loved ones or a therapist, tend to want to "stuff", or "avoid" their feelings because they are volatile.

The importance of a mother to a child is undoubtedly significant. Of course, both parents, have an impact on the development of a child. Yet, there are some unique attributes to each. It is safe to say the distinguishing role as a carrier of life is pretty unique. That alone illustrates the significance of the role that a mother plays in a child's life. While in vitro, meaning still in the womb, a mother houses the entire miraculous development of a child. Her influence on the ongoing development of that child remains throughout their life span. If we assessed the various tasks a mother typically acts out on a daily basis with

her child(ren), we are able to see that the contributions affect every area of development, especially emotional and social. For example, when a mother nurtures her infant by attending to its various cries of hunger, cold or hot temperature, and sleepiness she is

Death ends a life. Not a relationship."

Mitch Albom

instilling a level of emotional security that the infant needs to feel safe and cared for. These early nurturing tasks have lasting effects for the bond as parent and child itself, in addition to how the child will relate to everyone else he/she encounters as well as the world.

It is no wonder that the role of a parent (a mother in particular) is considered one of the toughest jobs a person can ever have. I've served numerous men and women with a range of presenting concerns. They come to me to help them for various reasons, oftentimes not initially described as an issue with their mother. Yet, they often have to deal with unresolved 'stuff' with their mothers to resolve and/or better manage whatever issue they thought would be the focus of therapy. Similarly, if the role of a mother is that influential to a person's life, so is the role of her death. There's a quote by Mitch Albom that says, *"Death ends a life. Not a relationship."*

[Pause with me for a second to really consider these words.]

Be present with what it is saying. For those unfamiliar, this is considered in the therapy world as practicing mindfulness. Mindfulness, is taking time to focus our thoughts only on what and/or who is there in the moment, not in the past nor the future. As you read that quote, be in touch with the feeling(s) it evokes within. Not sure? If you have to keep repeating the quote. Try your best to determine the feelings that stir inside of you as you read it. Try your best to describe it. This is important because it could enlighten you to what your authentic relationship with your loss is at this time. In other words, how you are experiencing the loss in the innermost part of you. For example, if you were saddened reading the quote it is likely that you primarily relate to the loss with sadness, perhaps even in a depressive manner.

Now is probably a good time to clear up a misconception about sadness in response to bereavement and sadness as an indicator of a pathological condition, such as a depressive disorder. It is common for sadness to be a part of the process of bereavement; that is, if the

...the closer the relationship the more difficult the loss and potentially the bereavement process altogether.

loved one was viewed in a loving and caring way - meaning there was a close relationship between the deceased and survivor(s). In fact, the closer the relationship the more difficult the loss and potentially the bereavement process altogether. Losing your mother, will undoubtedly come with emotional up and downs. Sometimes, those down periods may last more than two weeks. For example, in my experience I've worked with individuals who have lost their mothers in close proximity to their birthday, which is in close proximity to a holiday that happens to be around the same date of another significant loss. In short they experience several loss triggers in consecutive years. This can result in sadness for several weeks for them.

Let's be honest, there's only so much loss one can handle. Despite this, a diagnosis of Depression may not be appropriate. Actually, labeling bereavement as depression when it is not appropriate may be more damaging than helpful. Especially if someone begins to take antidepressants and does not need to. In general, sadness or depressive like symptoms (i.e. fatigue, poor sleep, crying spells, etc.) during bereavement may be prolonged, but the symptoms can subside and are not typically accompanied by a feeling of 'emptiness' or suicidal thoughts like those that would be present in the case of Major Depression Disorder.

Referring back to the brief exercise mentioned earlier. Perhaps sadness was not the initial feeling or emotion evoked in you upon reading the quote. If I were to be transparent, the first time I read it, it stirred me up and evoked an internal conflict between logic and my emotional self including feelings of frustration and longing.

Maybe you were like me and not able to identify just one. If you could not identify any, readily, that is okay. You may need practice getting in touch with that part of you, just keep trying. Awareness will be a helpful part of this journey. The following models of grief can prove to be useful as well. I like to think of it this way - "The more you know, the greater potential to grow." We can grow despite the grief and in the midst of adjusting to the loss of our mothers.

The stages of grief, as first introduced by grief pioneer Dr. Kubler-Ross in her book, On Death and Dying, captured her observations of patients that were dying and the emotional responses that they experienced. She did not intend for it to be used as an exact science or base of knowledge for treating 'stages' of grief, yet it has validity in that the following emotions can be experienced by those directly and indirectly affected by death and dying:

1) **Denial** - an emotional response that is most associated with disbelief or an unacceptance of the death, whether it is the anticipation of the death or in actuality.

2) **Anger** - an emotional response that is most associated with frustration or resentment toward the reality of the death.

3) **Bargaining** – the tendency for one to respond to the loss in a manner that attempts to change the outcome of death by hypothetically changing their own behavior.

4) **Depression** - when the loss has been acknowledged and results in

various psychological symptoms such as poor sleep and/or appetite, frequent crying spells, and even irritability. Individuals in this "stage" are likely the most common for those that enter into grief and bereavement counseling.

5) **Acceptance** - the state of coming to terms with the loss; no longer denying it happened or trying to change its outcome. Grief and bereavement counseling can help facilitate this stage for those that may have difficulty doing so.

Again, don't consider these 'stages' as an exact science, but as a tool that can promote greater awareness of where you are in your process. Awareness is a big deal in the sense that if you can be aware of what is going on within yourself, you can then determine what you can do to get to where you want to be. There's another stage model that can provide insight and understanding to all of this.

Apparently, there were people BEFORE Kubler-Ross that had some thoughts on grief. John Bowlby and Collin Parkes were there before her, with their own ideas about what this grief thing is about. Bowlby was a psychologist that focused on the attachments between a child and its primary caregivers. He determined that grief has to do with dealing with losing the attachment that existed in the relationship once one person has died. He initially put this in a three stage model and Parkes added the fourth and last stage. The stages may look familiar as they actually provided a foundation for many models that came after, including Kubler-

Ross' five stage model. Review the four stages of Bowlby and Parkes and see if any appear relevant in your process.

Stage 1: Shock and numbness

During this stage, death does not feel real and it is impossible to accept. This stage includes physical (somatic) symptoms, such as: headaches, common cold, body soreness, etc. There is a risk of shutting down and the inability to communicate feelings and thoughts. You may get stuck and not be able to progress to the other phases of grief.

Stage 2: Yearning and Searching

You are aware of the void left behind from the death. Also, awareness that the future you imagined, (that they would be a part of it), will not happen. There is a desperate attempt to obtain the comfort they once provided. There may be a level of preoccupation that exists. For example, visiting the gravesite on a daily basis.

Stage 3: Despair and Disorganization

You are accepting that everything has changed and that it will not got back to the way it used to be. Despite this acceptance there are feelings of hopelessness and anger. It will feel like life won't improve and the future does not look good without their presence.

Stage 4: Reorganization and Recovery

In this stage you begin to have a restored outlook on life; able to see positivity in the future. As a result, you rebuild yourself and the environment you are in. Bowlby believed at this stage the death can still influence one, but will no longer be at the forefront of our thoughts.

You will notice that relating to any one of these stages, no matter the model, include identifying with a dominant feeling at any given point of mourning, at any given time. Yet, there are other factors that can contribute to how we "feel" about losing our moms in supplement to the cold reality of her absence. It can also depend on the circumstances surrounding her passing and other factors.

(2)

"In my feelings…"

As aforementioned, grief is the internal thoughts and feelings that one experiences in response to a loss. When you lose your mother you will likely experience a wide spectrum of feelings. Many of which only you will primarily be aware of. That is if you allow yourself to be present with those feelings or thoughts. I would highly encourage you to do so, unless you tend to feel flooded by your emotions. A flooding of emotion means that you are experiencing them in a manner that is intense, overwhelming, and potentially long in duration. Flooding can impede the healing process because oftentimes it doesn't feel safe. This is not ideal because our natural instinct is to remain safe at all cost emotionally; the same as we would protect ourselves physically from danger.

When we feel threatened (even by our own emotions) we are left with a choice to *"fight"*, *"flight"*, or *"freeze"* from them. Anger like feelings such as rage, frustration, and criticism can prompt a desire to "fight" in a loss situation. Feelings like denial, abandonment, and quilt could evoke a notion to take "flight" from being present with the death. We can become paralyzed or "freeze" in response to the loss when we feel anxious, overwhelmed, and lonely.

My mom was possibly one of the strongest persons I knew. She was also equally just as sensitive and one of the most sensitive persons I knew. I have pondered and attempted to determine if there's a direct correlation between the two. I cannot say for sure, but I settle on the belief she had to be strong to cope with her sensitivity. I can say for certain that she cared immensely about just about everything and everyone (mostly). This made her vulnerable to getting her feelings hurt.

In my experience, "sensitive" is viewed as a negative characteristic and those who are labeled as such can be made to feel bad for being *sensitive.* To be honest, I can be sensitive in certain situations. Yet, should someone who is emotionally reactive or impacted more easily then the 'average' person be ridiculed for it? For feelings are meant to be felt and communicate our present needs (actual or perceived). We all can guess what happens to any of us that have needs that go unmet for an extended time. It probably won't be pretty. Nonetheless, to be fair, Ma had been through a lot in her 58 years alive, which contributed to her sensitive interpretations of criticism, judgments, etc. Therefore, I had to learn not to view it as a negative mark on her character, but understand through which lens she would view life situations at times - past hurt and wounds. To her credit, my mom evolved to a place of increasing awareness and insight about wrongdoings toward her in the form of *what others said and did was not to always be taken personally or as an attack on her*. That was indeed a process for her and I credit and am thankful to her for modeling the importance to seek therapy and to rely on resiliency factors, such as faith and church. It were those resiliency factors that helped her be far less impulsive and intuitive, which ultimately gave her the confidence to respond differently.

I believe the evidence of this area of personal growth for my mother birthed another common statement she came to frequently use, *'I'm in my feelings'*. When she would say that, it was to acknowledge that in the moment she was in process; that she had been triggered to feel some emotion that needed to be reconciled, until she determined how she would respond or if she would respond at all. She may have also said it to give herself permission that that was her response to whatever the trigger was and it was the best she could do at that time. In the past, Ma's automatic responses in an anger state would be to become explosive. Knowing this, allowing herself to be "in her feelings" was a big deal for her as it utilized those sort of anger management skills. It was indeed progressive for her and I can't help but to be proud of that.

Needless to say, my mom's actions were useful in my own process in dealing with her death and certain life challenges since her death. It provided a model of how to respond in highly emotional situations especially hurtful ones. In summary, that model consists of **1) increased awareness of triggers 2) insight to how those triggers evoke negative emotional responses 3) acknowledge that response and reconcile your part first, and 4) take further action, when appropriate.**

*****

There are different forms of grief that can compound, exaggerate, and increase the intensity of emotions we feel such as anticipatory, complicated, and vicarious grief. Individuals that may feel "stuck" in the grief process may be in part to being in a situation where one of the aforementioned forms of grief exist. Recall my earlier narrative on the time leading up to Ma's passing. At that time, I didn't know I was experiencing anticipatory grief. I do know now that anticipatory grief had me all '*in my feelings*'.

"...now I can go see what is wrong with me...I think it's cancer."

Ma

Anticipatory grief is a time when a loved one's death is assumed inevitable. For example, an individual and/or a their loved one that is diagnosed with a terminal illness such as stage 4 cancer could find themselves experiencing anticipatory grief. Actually, the onset of this form of grief can occur even when a diagnosis of that magnitude is simply suspected. It is in part why some individuals may choose to avoid seeking medical testing or help. My maternal grandmother, Sandra, transitioned the December prior to my mom. I remember after the funeral Ma telling me that she would "...now I can go see what is wrong with me...I think it's cancer." I immediately, denounced her suspicions. However, just a few months later, the testing was complete and it was ultimately confirmed. She had pancreatic cancer.

I remained in denial. I have always been an extremely optimistic and faith filled person. Perhaps in that situation, it was to a fault. My mom, was always strong in her faith as well, but she took on a rather logical position in this situation. Talk about irritating. I would become quite frustrated with her in the tense times post diagnosis. Although, in retrospect, I wondered how the loss of her own mother just a few months prior to being diagnoses influenced her seemingly accepting stance of being terminally ill. I wondered if it provided a level of comfort knowing she would see her mom again.

In my denial, I would initiate discussions on future plans with her. She would listen, with a few remarks of contemplation. Well, I remained in denial for quite some time to the extent that I rarely to never was aware of the significance of what it meant that she used to be talkative and opinionated and had started becoming increasingly contemplative and acquiescing. There came a time where denying my mom would die appeared to no longer be an option. So, I happily replaced it with, what else, but anger.

One of my many regrets that I eventually had to resolve was being so angry that at one-point Ma had to ask, "Are you mad at me?" My knee jerk and untruthful response was, 'No." The tumultuous responses of my own anticipatory grief experiences were founded in the fact that the months leading up to her diagnosis to the time of her transition, I was simultaneously experiencing numerous changes. I had just recently married, conceived my first child, bought a new home, and eventually gave birth. The mixture of all of that, while dealing with mom's illness, affected me in every way.

Anticipatory grief is not solely about the physical death. Now that the anticipated loss is a possibility, we begin to grieve all the secondary losses leading up to the death. My mom's decline of health prevented her from being her usual festive self; from being with me when her grandchild was being born; or even seeing him and our new home immediately, as I know she would have under normal health conditions. The key thing to remember is anticipatory grief is just that; the grief of things we lose and will lose, that occurs before our loved one passes on and leaves us in the physical form. Its complexities have something to do with the state of our thought process, the nature of our experiences leading up to death, and the role we play for our mothers during that time. In my personal and professional experience the factors that influence the experience of anticipatory grief can also determine if you will experience complicated grief in response to your mother's death.

Complicated grief is an emotional response that worsens and intensifies as time goes on. Although grief cannot be put on a timer, in general, many survivors of a death will eventually experience it with less and less negative emotions. Yet for some, that is not the case. Others can experience grief that is prolonged. This is what is known as complicated grief.

Complicated grief can be a real threat for those that lose their mothers unexpectedly, for anyone that served as the primary caretaker for her prior to death, or for anyone who has had limited experiences with loss or a significant history of losses. If we dare to find a positive for anticipatory grief, it is that it allows for the opportunity to "prepare." I use that word lightly. It is safe to say that rarely will one be fully prepared for losing a mom, but it can be attempted at least. However, for those whose mothers died unexpectedly, their survivors can be left feeling cheated out of a goodbye.

"It is safe to say that rarely will one be fully prepared for losing a mom."

In working with grieving spouses and children, I have heard several accounts of this happening and resulting in this form of grief. An unexpected death of a mother, can reap numerous regrets. These regrets, if unresolved, can perpetuate an intense grief experience and cause it to worsen. Although, one might be able to function in general with these regrets, there can come a point where one or more areas of functioning will be impaired.

It's worth mentioning that although regret seems to imply that there may have been strain or estrangement in the relationship, this is not necessarily true. In many cases, in fact, the relationship between the Survivor and his or her mother is likely indicative of the closeness in that relationship. Complicated grief is accompanied by an immense yearning and longing for the relationship that once was and fuels the grief, turned complicated. Since the events and variables leading up to death can be traumatic, even if only in its abrupt occurrence, complicated grief can be very challenging to overcome. This is significant because in many instances, human instinct tells us to be resilient and adapt. Complicated grief will likely require special care, if not specialized therapeutic intervention.

Vicarious grief, also known as vicarious bereavement, is a unique form of loss. This particular dynamic has to do with being emotionally, psychologically, or physically impacted by a loss that might not be directly your own. By losing someone significant to you such as a mother, vicarious loss or bereavement, can be felt more intensely or obviously. You may be experiencing this if you find yourself anxious, constantly thinking about or experiencing prolonged sadness, have seen a decrease in functionality (personally, academically, physically, socially, and/or in your career); or have become sensitive to the news or current events as a result of a loss. For example, consider the number of people that can be identified as experiencing grief in the aftermath of 9/11, or from any one of the mass school shootings, or shootings against black males by members of law enforcement. Of course, the close and immediate friends and family grieve the individuals lost from those tragedies, but the loss extends beyond those with close connection to them making it vicarious. This can also be a common occurrence for helping professionals, since they are exposed to tragedies and trauma by serving people that have endured such losses and challenges. Likewise, most of the aforementioned symptoms that accompany vicarious grief/bereavement are not isolated to just those who lose loved ones in their own family but those in the community and world. Once a person connects psychologically and emotionally with a situation of loss, grief is relevant and will require a grieving or bereavement process to adjust and hopefully adapt to any void that exists.

To lose a mother is devastating and the probability that you are vulnerable to community (local and the world) is fairly high. Therefore, when you attempt to assess your own grief or bereavement I encourage that this dynamic is kept in consideration. It will be a relevant factor in the assessment to what will be the necessary coping skills that are beneficial to promote your psychological, emotional, and mental well-being in addition to your self-care needs.

(3)

"I can't rob you of your feelings."

"I can't rob you of your feelings…" Ma used to say this whenever she was confronted by a person or situation where emotions were pretty intense. This may have been when confronted by a friend that felt wronged by her. As expressed before, my mom usually had good intentions toward others but, she struggled with effective communication at times (to put it nicely). Ma learned to contemplate the complaints before reacting or responding in a manner that might make matters even worse. By doing so she was able to acknowledge the complaint, avoid becoming defensive, and allow herself time to reflect on her words and/or action. Eventually, corrective measures, such as an apology or changed behavior, would be made. Sometimes it was fairly immediate, at other times it would be quite a length of time.

I wish I could say that everyone you encounter in your grief will be as willing to accept the words and behaviors you exhibit as a result of the death, but I cannot. Both grief and mourning are individualized. Therefore, the expectations of how one should grieve can be just as varied. Even within the same family. When a person experiences the death of a loved one, there are many variables to consider that can influence other's perception of what is an 'acceptable' response to that death. Here are a few:

- What age was the person at time of death?
- Were they a "good" or "bad" person?
- What was the relationship dynamic between the two of you?
- How did they die?

Based on the answers, you might be judged on how you grieve the loss. Unfortunately, Western/American culture has increasingly adopted the *'Get over it'*, *'He/She is in a better place...don't be sad'*, and *'You can't bring them back, so why cry about it?'* stance toward grief, that it can feel like it is wrong to mourn it. I assure you, it is not. There are some situations where grief can appear to be harmful to a person, such as someone not eating or drinking for dangerously long periods of time. In such a case, intervention for safety purposes might be necessary, but even then it would not be helpful for it to be from a place of judgment or with placement of expectations of societal norms. In bereavement, the feelings and thoughts are at the discretion of the bereaved. It is their right and privilege as it related to having a one of a kind connection to the deceased.

Allowing others, as well as ourselves, to experience their unique bereavement journey means to attempt to understand that we all have triggers that activate our connection to the loss. When activated those triggers will require attention, action, or both. Triggers can result in grief bursts, where you will find yourself overwhelmed with emotion that includes crying spells or feeling a distinct shift in mood. The occurrence of grief bursts might seem like they have no rhyme or reason. This is because on a typical day our conscious and unconscious mind are active. Therefore, you may be triggered in quite a hypersensitive way to the loss of your mother. The memories we hold of our experiences include all five senses: sight, hearing, smells, touch, and taste. Any one of the senses can be triggered to recall a particular memory that may incite a grief burst. For example, my mom loved music and dancing. I can recall when I would often be triggered by various songs to recall her memory or an experience we shared, and I'd become overcome with emotion. This is just an example of one of the senses being triggered. Think about it:

Sight – Pictures and/or places visited together

Hearing - A voice message still saved in your phone

Smell - The perfume she used to wear

Touch - A soft blanket or clothing she would wear

Taste - A favorite dish she used to cook

As you can see, losing a mom can provide a great possibility for triggering to occur in our day to day lives. When we are creating memories in present tense we are not mindful the effect they are having on our psyche. We can connect with the positive feeling(s) that is created from the experience but, we are rarely conscientious of its staying power or magnitude of impact. Unfortunately like most stress, the stress of losing a mother will expose that staying power and impact. Hence, grief bursts can happen at any time, especially around significant dates such as holidays, birthdays, and anniversaries tend to especially be difficult.

I must forewarn your, grief busts are sneaky. They will occur even if you may have dealt with the death of your mother, accepted her absence, and are back to the functioning life within your norm. One moment you can be just fine, and then boom; a grief burst will appear! I know there are some personalities that might be very unsettled by that. Also, different lifestyles and life circumstances might feel inconvenienced by grief burst's ability to put you back in the throes of your grief.

We have all heard, "time heals all wounds", a popular cliché that comes up quite often in bereavement as it pertains to the death of a loved one. I gently encourage you not to take too much stock in that. Instead I'd like to gently encourage for you to take adequate time, even if at designated times, to manage your hurt. Whether your mom died weeks, months, years, or even decades ago, there may still be times when you feel immense sadness. For example, you may feel it on a holiday such as Mother's Day. Think about it, holidays typically spent in a time of a reflection and showing appreciation, can foster intense triggers to loss. It depends on several variables whether your sense of loss will be more intense sometimes versus a manageable task. There's no exact science to it. If you try to "figure it out" you'll continue on being very frustrated. A more beneficial approach that can be helpful is to be present with the pain, meaning you are acknowledging its presence.

When you're present, or mindful of your pain, you are better able to be in awareness of your needs for that particular time. With that awareness, you're better able to seek out or request the assistance you need, such as social support and/or resources that you can use to help get you through the challenge of bereavement. Don't forget to always be compassionate towards yourself and to give yourself permission to feel the feelings you are having, in real-time.

In my personal and professional experience exhibiting compassion towards yourself is a priceless intervention. It's an intervention that will foster and promote feelings of comfort in its own right. There's something to say about the benefit of being comforted while in mourning because it provides purity and safety. When that approach toward your individual mourning journey feels like it has been compromised and the idea of your mother's absence feels too unbearable, the need for emotional/psychological safety can appear to be in jeopardy. If this happens, consider giving yourself a time limit to "be in your feelings". Of course, this might mean resisting a flight response to avoid the pain and reality that your mom is no longer with you, because you also no longer want to experience the pain with raw and unbridled intensity. Perhaps, putting your pain on the clock, can aid in building up to a place that feels less overwhelming.

To put your 'pain on a clock', first determine a reasonable time frame, maybe an hour. In that hour, symptoms that include sadness, anxiety, low motivation, and tearfulness can be allowed to persist without guilt, shame, or judgement. When that hour, or whatever predetermined time has concluded take the liberty to function as you normally would. This can be helpful because it facilitates a process of mourning in spurts instead of breaking down in a manner that is undesirable.

Similarly, let this be a call to action for all of us that serve as support to someone in grief at some point. Don't rob these persons of their feelings, but instead encourage and try to empathize with their experience. That will foster an opportunity for them to take the brave step into the mourning process when they are ready. It is not a coincidence that people find themselves stuck in grief, despite the modern time urging of "get over it...don't feel that way...don't think that way... etc."

This is a very common issue when people come to me for grief issues. In essence, they feel uncomfortable with their own feelings about the grief they are experiencing. Oftentimes, this uncomforting feeling is due to how others have made them feel about their authentic feelings toward the loss and the pressure from work or society to feel differently and get back to normal. Getting back to "normal" is their initial goal for therapy. However, with the onset of grief I have found that meeting them where they are and fostering a safe environment to be real about their feelings is a more beneficial goal.

Now consider the stages of grief, again. It is possible for the discomfort with the grief to come from an internal conflict and not only the external influence of cultural norms and our social supports. You may not believe it, but not only do we have to give ourselves permission to be present with our grief, (which will then free us to mourn), we have to deal with others who say it is wrong even when we are at odd with our own feelings. I have observed this frequently when there is an internal conflict about harboring ill feelings toward the deceased.

Here's an example for several of the 'stages' that may help you determine if you or someone you know may be struggling with this particular grief dynamic:

Denial: She would not leave me, she is just on vacation.

Anger: How could she leave me?!

Bargaining: If only she would have just told me she was sick sooner.

Depression: She's really gone, how will I go on?

Acceptance: She's gone. Somehow I will adjust.

DENIAL

If there is **denial** at the root of the bereavement impasse than it is helpful to explore the significance of the deceased. At first consideration, it may appear that denial is an unhealthy reaction. However, denial can serve an awesome purpose; one that protects us from becoming too overwhelmed with the permanent reality of the loss. We cannot rob someone of their denial, lest we prematurely provide support or intervention and as a result, prolong or further impede the potential for acceptance. Please keep in mind that it is possible that simply the idea of the death of a loved one can be too much to bear for some.

ANGER

In many cases, **anger** toward the deceased can stifle the ability to be at peace with the death. When there is primarily anger, the seeds of resentment and/or shame and guilt can grow. This growth is like weeds in a garden; it serves a purpose, but for the most it doesn't portray the desired result. In short, sometimes we have unresolved issues with loved ones that die, especially when the death is unexpected or happens so rapidly, our emotions could not catch up. While the anger is indicative of the intensity of love toward the loss it will have to be acknowledged and addressed. Anger is an easy emotion to have, as it is typically one we all can feel. Still it can be just as scary or undesirable. Not to mention, how does one resolve anger with someone that is not around to talk to or confront?

In therapy, resolving anger with someone who is deceased is done in a variety of ways such as processing the authentic feelings in the form of their narrative: writing a letter to the loved one, role play and act out the confrontation (also known as the empty chair exercise), keeping an anger journal, etc. These are just a few techniques. The important thing is to confront the anger and not allow any guilt or shame for holding anger toward a deceased person prevent you from the important work of reconciling the root of the anger. Anger is sometimes described as a secondary emotion, which basically means it is a mask for a more vulnerable feeling like hurt or despair. Unfortunately, to mourn is to be vulnerable. It can be helpful to consider mourning as an expressive gift of love that keeps giving.

BARGAINING

We will often find ourselves in a state of **bargaining** when we lose a mother, and we can be angry while doing it. Recall, that in bargaining we are looking to change the outcome of the death. In doing so, we might place blame on ourselves and even them. Blame can come from a place of anger.

It can be helpful to consider mourning as an expressive gift of love that keeps giving."

It seeks to make someone responsible for an outcome we do not desire. It can also be an attempt to make someone or something take responsibility for the undesirable.

Bargaining can speak to a need to redeem control as a reaction to the mysterious power that death possesses. A death will prompt us to explore existential dilemmas, which tends to be in the grey area of understanding versus the black and white distinction that death has. Existential dilemmas prompt questioning along the lines of: Is there life after death? What is the meaning of life? What is my purpose? Similarly to denial and anger responses, bargaining, is another form of coping to the loss.

DEPRESSION

When we find ourselves in a **depressive** state, we are usually in a state of mind that is processing the reality of the death in a way that primarily creates feelings of sadness, despair, and uncertainty. The depression is indicative that we are still having difficulty with the idea of finding a new norm, because we wish for yesterday when they were still here. In my experience as a therapist, this is the most common reason clients seek out help. They have experienced a loss and subsequently begin to exhibit depressive like symptoms. Please note, however, that the presentation of symptoms that appear to be depressive does not automatically denote a diagnosis of Depression, the actual disorder. Sure, it can lead to that, but it is not always the case initially.

It can feel like a daunting task trying to establish a "new norm." It is worth mentioning again that a new norm is the process of reconciling cognitive and behavioral needs that were met by your mother when she was alive and learning how to manage those needs without her. Reconciling those needs can be tough. As humans, we are creatures of habit and can be quite resistant to change. Losing a mother is a huge change to adjust to. However, making that adjustment is possible and a primary task for improving depressive like symptoms. For example, if your mother was a key emotional support for you whenever you were stressed or needed advice, it will be helpful to increase your social supports to provide that emotional support in the future due to her absence. Although, you may not view the two to share equal value, it will hopefully allow the loss to be better managed. In no way am I suggesting that you go in search of a replacement for your mom, because that would be an impossible mission. I simply recommend such actions as a way to cope with a notable void.

ACCEPTANCE

Accepting the loss occurs when the reality that your mom is no longer living and you aren't just having a bad dream has settled in both cognitively and emotionally. Yes, there will still be grief bursts and emotionally challenging days. No, you won't have to forget about her love and life with you. When you are ready for this part of the journey, it will consist of an adaptation process. Life is forever changed when a mother dies. Officially, from the day it happens, your way of life will change. To accept that is to accept that you are now engaging into a process of adapting to the different landscapes of your life. Accepting that does not indicate you should no longer miss her presence, but that you are intentional about learning how to live and be adequately able to function in your various roles in her absence. My personal motivation that I extend as a sincere hope for each of us experiencing mother loss, is that in adapting to your changed worlds there are things that reveal themselves to then be used for the purpose of attaining the best that life has to offer.

(4)

"More will be revealed."

Ma was a people person. She was an extrovert on steroids to be honest. I recall the time she mentioned that in her youth, friends and family would often compare her to the 1970's singer/dancer/actress Lola Falana. Of course at the time and being of a tender age, I had no idea who that was, but apparently that was a comparison to be proud of. Her people skills usually put her in a position to be the advisor, confidant, sponsor, mentor, and friend to many. Most of the time she loved serving in those capacities. Yet, there were times that the extent of her advice or insight would be simply put into these four words...'more will be revealed'.

Whether the context of her words were in a joking manner or in an effort to decrease the other person's anxiety, per usual, she was right.

Allow me to belabor the significance of this particular saying for a moment longer. First of all, we all might be familiar with the personality type(s) and sense of purpose that can be assigned to a person that voluntarily serves others in a leadership capacity. Character traits such as a good listener, strategic, responsible and dependable are important for a leader to have and it doesn't matter whether the support be emotional, physical, financial, etc. I believe leadership adequately describes the various roles my mom held in her life and for the people she loved and cared for. Honestly, she would take lead in most situations - sometimes without being asked. That is the type of woman she was. So, it is interesting and inspiring at the same time that she would have the capacity to yield to a question, dilemma, or situation with simply, "More will be revealed…"

Of course, some situations are more complex than others and to respond in such a manner may be more avoidant than accepting of the situation. However, let's focus on the accepting side of it, shall we? Again, Ma was a leader, a take charge individual, and a stereotypical New Yorker in some aspects. (I apologize if you are from New York and reading this. I make that statement from a loving place.) Back to Ma… In essence, that is why it is so significant that this saying and life approach from her is taken as a memorable lesson she (unknowingly) taught me. In modeling her ability to accept or respond to something that required more information and the patience to wait for it, she left an emotional inheritance I could and have used in my mourning process. Grief, Loss, and Bereavement will all be accompanied by "why", "what about", "how", and the like, questioning. This is natural due to our expectation, albeit unrealistic, to figure death out. When these sort of questions present, (it is dependent on what your unique journey looks like), but they will present in most or all cases. Some of us may be better at managing or reconciling them than others. Expect them occur, that is assuming they are not already happening to you.

Personally, I had my share of questions and attempts to figure out why MY MOM had to die (if you couldn't tell already from just reading the introduction to this book). In fact, these moments would come in waves based on what "stage" I was in at that given time. It was not until I reflected and decided to adopt an approach that *"more will be revealed"*, that the waves decreased in duration and at times, intensity. By taking this saying to heart, I was able to feel gratitude, not that Ma was gone, but that she told me that there would be situations and times that this thought would be the best, perhaps only, answer available to me, and to be okay with that. Trust me, I still have my moments. In particular, those moments occur when I begin to compare my life to others. You know that moment when you are on social media, or at a store or restaurant, and see mothers and daughters enjoying each other's company, meanwhile you only have memories.

Ironically, it has been reflecting on memories of my mom's contribution to my life while she was here that helped identify the insights

I needed then, also has helped me adapt to her absence now. In that process, there is contrasting activity at play. Somehow, while I connect with Ma by living out the wisdom and principles inherited from her life, I am simultaneously able to better adapt to losing her. It is a guiding light from beyond, if you will. In adopting this as a life principle in my mourning process and as a way of coping, I recognize several other means of facilitating an ongoing connection with our mothers. For example, the act of saying their names whenever we get the chance.

I recall the first time I had a client to present with bereavement issues and I asked for the name of the loved one that passed. I had no idea how that question, stated with the most intellectual intention, would be answered in a manner that carried an observable sense of relief and what I can only discern as gratitude. I learned a very important lesson that day and that was to have persons that are bereaved and mourning a loved one to say the name of who(m) they lost. I want to believe I knew the importance of names prior to that encounter, yet if I did, it was not to the extent of what I learned that day. In that moment, it was imprinted in my therapeutic tool belt and personal knowledge base, that to say the name of someone who has died is like an invitation for them to come alive once more in the hearts of the broken hearted.

Saying their names is an important invitation to provide because some of us, perhaps unconsciously or consciously, will disconnect from their names simply because they are no longer here physically. That is a disservice to the mourning process and the authentic feelings of love that we feel in our bereavement. Therefore, I encourage this practice and to speak their names as frequently as possible to obtain the emotional relief it can foster. Say their name to communicate any unspoken gratitude for them. In my experience, bereaved clients will say their loved one's name with anticipation. It becomes their way of saying thank you and to express love and adoration. Who says those feelings have to be withheld just because she is "gone"? I encourage them to go ahead and acknowledge that person's importance and relevance in their life.

Unfortunately, the opportunities to speak about our moms' names may be limited because our supports may feel uncomfortable with discussing them. Let's be honest, death is an uncomfortable topic for most people. It sure was for me at one time. Couple that with the shame and guilt that they may carry for not knowing what the heck to say to us because again, how HUGE is it to lose a mom, right?! Trust me, friends and family know that and it can feel helpless. So, what do people do when they feel shame, guilt, and helplessness? Run in the opposite direction of whatever is causing it.

You may understand this, but it can be just as difficult to accept it, because that discomfort and avoidance of allowing you to reflect on the loss of your mom can lead to a feeling of intense loneliness. When there is an influence, internal or external to avoid these moments of reflection, we are denied a major contributing factor to our healing and the adaptation process of mourning. In therapy, I encourage and prompt clients to freely speak their mother's name as often as possible. If for some reason there is apprehension or resistance to doing so, no need to push it. But, there is comfort to be found in that practice. Names are important. It is one of the very first rituals we use to assign value to our relationships and the connection we have with a person. Isn't that why parents give so much thought and attention to the pursuit of finding the 'perfect' name for their unborn child?

Names are representations of who we are, whose we are, and where we came from. They also are believed to help in molding the identity that we will have. That being said, to refuse to say or address someone by their name while alive would be of utmost disrespect. Therefore, to speak upon and say the name of our moms in their memory is a testament to our respect and love for them.

Another way I have encountered the truth behind the wisdom of, *'more will be revealed'*, in respect to loss and bereavement, is when I think about my relationship with my mom and how it changed upon her passing. In truth, our relationship had already begun to look different prior to her passing, due to me becoming a new mother just months before. Shortly after giving birth to my son as I became acclimated to the new role of being a primary source of love, nurturing, safety, and nutrients for him I gained a greater understanding and appreciation for my mom. My eyes were opened and my perspective started to shift on what I once perceived as her parenting shortcomings. I realized that whatever shortcomings she may have had were a result of being human, and that there really isn't a handbook for being a perfect mother.

As priorities in my life were revolutionized because I was now a mother myself, I had so many revelations. Like why she hugged me so hard every time she seen me. Or why as a child I couldn't stay the night or even play with any and everybody in the neighbor. Or why I could not miss school unless it required an immediate doctor or emergency room visit. Becoming a mother showed me the type of love that drives me to love and protect my child in a way I have never wanted to for anyone else in my life before. I learned that is all my mom probably ever wanted to do for my siblings and me. These realizations changed me as a daughter and ultimately how I related to and wanted to connect with my mom.

According to popular human development models, including Erik Erikson's, individual development, from birth to adulthood, should consist of achieving tasks successfully between childhood and becoming an adult so that one's identity from their parents is distinguishable. To do so is a sort of cumulative goal toward independence. During the separation process a child can easily find themselves consciously and unconsciously view their parent, not as an actual person, but only as an authority figure. Typically, this leads to misjudging who our parents really are in their fullness (i.e. human and hero) and instead they are viewed extremely flat and one-sided (i.e. human OR hero). Authority figures, including parents, tend to be perceived and viewed based on the words and actions they make due to the impact it has on those directly impacted by them. They rarely get the luxury of empathy and understanding. Typically, children idealize their parents to demonize them as adolescents. In adulthood things begin to come into balance. When a child becomes a parent themselves a shift takes place. In fact, the shift will likely begin prior to that, like when entering into adulthood as a child gains more independence and strives to achieve stability on their own. A good example of this is when a young adult leaves the home to work or go to college and has to pay their own bills. As if a switch turns on, they might immediately begin to understand and possibly appreciate their parents' rules and boundaries for household expenses and spending. Of course, this is a general analysis and there are several variables that might create an entirely different dynamic for some.

I can speak to appreciating my mom as a parent because oftentimes, she included me in her decision making, as well as, communicated the importance of the life skills she wanted to instill in me. I still primarily viewed her as super authority "MOM" versus, Gail, a woman trying to figure out this thing called life just like the rest of us. In hindsight, I have laughed at myself for the extent of how much my views have shifted since finding out about her terminal diagnosis of Pancreatic Cancer. Despite the countless reflections I have made since her passing, I can recall almost the exact moment when my view of my mom changed; where I focused on her as her own person and not just, my mom – the parent. Almost poetically my view of her changed again during her last body viewing, a day prior to the funeral, as I sat back in observation of those paying their last respects to her and watching the Celebration of Life slideshow her longtime friend and skilled photographer, Ron, created for her. It switched something on inside me. That "something" that I can best describe as an 'aha' moment, was inspired by a video clip in the slideshow that captured her dancing by herself without a care or concern for anything or anyone. It was such a befitting moment to capture for the slideshow of her life because she loved to dance. My mom loved to dance. Gail loved to dance, and that image made it clear that she was both. Also, seeing that clip brought back several memories of her in dance throughout my life. Being privy to the trials and tribulations she endured and overcame in her life, that dancing video clip felt comforting, as if she was there herself prompting all of us there to dance in our own lives, including times of difficulty and sadness.

It may seem odd that a relationship can exist with someone that has died, but I have to say that it's very possible and the relationship may even be in stark contrast to when the person was alive. Apparently, there are phases to it and its part of the individual process of bereavement and mourning. Now it seems to be more like a harmonious dance between the two, person and parent that has only increased my appreciation love and admiration toward her. As a result, my approach to connecting with her is increasingly well rounded. This connection makes me beam with a newfound pride to be her second child. When reconciling our previous relationship dynamics there were times I would feel regretful for not seeing her in that light sooner. Thankfully, it does not take away from our current relationship. If you struggle with regret or guilt, know that no one is perfect and try to find a way to be present, to process, and eventually progress by releasing yourself from those emotions.

Relationship is defined as the state of being connected. When our moms were alive we were connected physically, emotionally, and mentally. When separation is a matter of death, the relationship might be less connection in a physical sense, but the other forms of connection is still there. For those of us with spiritual beliefs, the physical absence magnifies a spiritual connection that can maintain an intimacy between us and our mothers. It has for me. In short, information and experiences we attach to persons we love will influence the connection we have with them. I hope that makes sense. The information and experiences that we gain post-mortem about our mothers can have an enormous impact on the connection with them. While mourning them learn to adapt to their absence. So, fear not, even though resistance to mourning the loss of a loved one, out of a fearful assumption that mourning equates to moving on when 'moving on' equals a need to forget. Although, it is understandable how one can come to that conclusion, it is

Connections and relationships simply change and do not have to end.

not true. Connections and relationships simply change and do not have to end. As the dynamic of that relationship is reconfigured, there is a new normal that develops.

In the circle of life, people are born and people pass away. Both life events come with their own innate sense of mystery. In fact, spiritual, philosophical, and existential questions in part are frequently prompted by the mysterious nature a loss. It can be hypothesized that death and the subsequent questioning in its aftermath is a contributing factor to the emotional impact of losing a loved one; especially a significant loss such as one's mother. Whether or not there are answers to any of those questions, when loss has made an imprint on your life it presents a necessary truth that a new norm will need to be established. Truth or not, establishing a new norm can come with ease for some and can be very challenging for others. The concept of a new norm has to do with the immediate and/or inevitable changes we will encounter when are mothers are no longer with us. These changes will vary and range according to the nature of the relationship between the two of you.

(5)

"Say thank you..."

Gratitude is defined as "the quality of being thankful". I understand that being thankful and the task of mourning the death of a mother may seem to make an odd pair. What could one possibly be thankful about while trying to make sense of losing the mother they cared for and loved? Especially when the reality is that she will never speak to you again, hug you again, or provide the support you will most definitely need at some point during the remainder of your own days. It's quite a bit to wrap one's mind around, let alone begin to think about saying 'thank you' for anything, especially during the initial time period following their passing. There may be some whom this concept may come easily to. For most of us it will not, at least in the immediate time period after our mother's die. Perhaps, especially after a mother dies.

In my case, I am hard pressed to separate thankfulness and Ma, even now. Reason being, I heard my mom say and prompt the words 'thank you' so many times, I don't dare to count. In fact, she was so adamant about teaching me and my siblings to show our gratitude, appreciation, and thanks. She would allow us a whopping three seconds (maybe) after receiving anything from anyone before we would be met with, "Are you going to say thank you?" or "Did you say thank you?" or "Did you forget to say thank you?" and several other variations of her expectation that we verbalize our gratitude at the very first opportunity available to do so.

In her eyes, no matter the time or circumstance, we should give our thanks with the utmost promptness. Also, she preferred that we expressed thanks multiple times versus saying it one time; more than sufficed for most people. It could be quite aggravating, and to say that this annoyed me would be an understatement. Eventually, I learned that it was in my best interest to simply give as much thanks as immediately as possible to avoid the interrogation that would ensue if she wasn't satisfied with implicit and explicit displays of indebtedness for whatever it is I was given. I learned that lesson so well, that it is probably why just seconds after witnessing my mom's last breath in this physical world, the first thing I remember saying was, "THANK YOU!

In reflection, it's hard to believe, but that 'Thank You' is indeed what I said. I was thankful that she was no longer in pain. The moment leading up to her transition from the physical world to the spiritual world still was indeed a sight to see; surreal even. In honesty, the verdict on whether that experience helped or hindered my mourning process changes from grief burst to grief burst. Nonetheless and since her passing, I have identified countless of reasons I have to be thankful to have had my mother for the time that I did. This is the reason I have to believe that one can grieve, mourn, and utilize death as a catalyst for an increased purpose to live. It's something I have identified as a process of going from a mourner to a MOREner.

"...going from a mourner to a MOREner."

Becoming a MOREner, relies on the shift from the external; actionable participation with the loss to utilizing it as fuel in a hope that motivates and drives a purpose in life that was not there prior to the loss. Or perhaps it was lying dormant and was awakened, if you will, from the death and the meaning attached to the loss. As the name reflects, a MOREner, is able to make "more" out of an absence of their loved one. It doesn't mean the loss is any less significant or painful, even. Yet, primarily, a MOREner will likely experience the loss with less sadness or anger than while grieving or even mourning.

Another Catch 22 in losing a mother or loved one is that on one hand you can be more appreciative of the loved ones that are still living.

Yet, on the other hand likely find yourself being more sensitive to other losses that follow - even if those losses are not in your immediate family, extended family, or social network. A duality of grief in a way, isn't it? I guess that is why it is said that 'experience is the best teacher'.

I can remember that before my mom passed, I was merely sympathetic to news of death. I merely felt sorry for the griever, but did not quite understand the pain they were in. This had a lot to do with the fact that I had very little experience with anyone close to me dying. By close, I mean anyone that I had any significant connection to. To grieve and eventually mourn is directly affected by the connection between both persons. Therefore, even when you have knowledge of or casual encounters with someone that dies the impact on your emotional state, in general, will be manageable. Of course, there are those exceptional exceptions such as when we, the general public, may be strongly affected by say a celebrity's death. Although, even in that exception, there's a connection with the celebrity made through their outreach with the general public and contribution to our culture and society that can account for a strong fandom grief response. With mom gone, I have become quite sensitive to the intense and tumultuous range of emotion one can have in response to a loss.

In contrast, I am almost equally attentive to the friends, family, clients, community leaders, etc. that I love and/or share connections with. Losing someone significant, like a mother or mother like figure, can provide an opportunity to take inventory of who is still present in your life to love, appreciate, celebrate, and even reconcile with. To do so can be a valuable way of coping. Ideally, the love and care will be reciprocated and provide a sense of connectedness that can replenish where loss has depleted.

In retrospect, Ma must have had her fair share of loss that I remained oblivious to or refused to take notice. Either way, I am aware that she was comfortable with

Gratitude can transcend a grave and is not bound by it.

mentioning or discussing her own immortality and the inevitability of death. I recall another saying she had, *"Give me my flowers now"*. In short, she wanted to be shown that she was appreciated and loved while she was still physically able to hear and hold such gestures. My siblings and I often dismissed her when she initiated the subject. To our defense and to give context, she made those sort of remarks decades prior to any evidence of health issues and definitely before her terminal diagnosis. Yet, one cannot help but acknowledge that it makes sense. I may not have got it then, but I get it now. Yes, losing a mother is an opportunity to reflect on the small and significant contributions she made in your life. By doing so, perhaps just perhaps it will prompt a smile, laugh, or comforting embrace in the form of a memory. Although, we may no longer be able to give our mothers their thanks in the form of flowers and they physically accept them, placing them at the gravesite of their final resting place or in your own home or space of choice can still symbolically represent your gratitude. It can be a beneficial mourning practice or ritual that many find comfort in. Ma loved sunflowers, so it's a linking object (more on this shortly) that I gravitate to in her honor. This principle can be extended to others who we find deserving of a "thank you". Once we are out of the tight grip of grief and in process of mourning we can find ourselves open to being increasingly more present with the environments and persons in our life. A common result of losing a mother is identifying with an increased significance of importance in the other relationships with the other parent, other primary caretakers (i.e. grandparent), siblings, extended family and friends. For those that have a relationship with their fathers, upon the death of their mother, may find themselves more dependent on that relationship. They cannot expect that their father compensate for the loss of a mother, but in many ways this is a normalized response to cope with losing her. That dependence is not only limited to the surviving parent. It is likely to happen to any and/or all the remaining relationships that a person holds of any value. Given that, the support of a father aids in the coping of the loss. As a person in mourning that support will be invaluable and can be an opportunity to extend the life principle of giving flowers while one is still alive to that and other supporters.

There are several accounts I can recall of people I have seen for grief that felt almost tormented that they were not able to verbalize their gratitude in the way they would have liked before their loved one passed. Such regrets can wreak emotional havoc on us, and oftentimes, mentally, physically, and spiritually. I am grateful to Ma for her reasonably "unusual' (in my previous naiveté) level of awareness and comfort with being immortal, that she established an expectation to appreciate and give thanks to her and others with little or no delay. Now that I know the true wisdom of that saying, I encourage everyone, even those with unsettled regret, to take this life principle and apply it. For some, it may feel "too late", but I challenge them in that it is never too late to say thank you. Gratitude can transcend a grave and is not bound by it. For those that want to thank their mothers who have since died, it can still be done, but may require creativity and flexibility.

Of course, those still here are definitely fair game. With death can come hard lessons. It is a frustrating and sad truth in some instances. However, it is an opportunity to grow as well, even when we feel we have mastered the relationships in our lives. Even if we believe that everyone that is deserving of our love and appreciation adequately receives such recognition. Say thank you for the little and big things you appreciate in your life; yourself included. Maybe give yourself some flowers, if you like that sort of thing. If not, do something that shows appreciation for your courage and best attempts at coping with a difficult situation, in this case - the loss of your mother.

In the world of psychology there are specific theories and corresponding techniques focused on gratitude. Many studies have shown the practice of gratitude has multiple benefits. Per a Harvard Health publication *In Praise of Gratitude*, "...gratitude is strongly and consistently associated with greater happiness. Gratitude helps people feel more positive emotions, relish good experiences, improve their health, deal with adversity, and build strong relationships." While mourning the loss of a mother, any one of these benefits would be helpful. Practicing gratitude can be facilitated in a variety of ways, such as reflecting on past memories that are viewed in a fond and positive manner; or intentionally being aware of the tangible and intangible possessions you may have on a daily basis (i.e. car, food, family support, health, etc.); or goals, opportunities, experiences you can look forward to. Understandably, some of us might have difficulty with this practice, in the immediate time of grief or altogether even. An "attitude of gratitude" as it is sometimes referred as, is not typically a natural or instinctive attitude we humans tend to have. In most cases, it is one that has to be nurtured and cultivated. Obviously, doing so after losing someone as significant as a mom, is not the ideal time, but it is possible. Try to encourage yourself to do what you can. Then try to do a little more the next time. Perhaps, starting out you simply write what you feel thankful for one minute or write down one thing today and try increasing it by one more thing each day.

(6)

"Who's here was supposed to be here."

Ma was a planner. She thrived when it came to making plans, no matter if it was for a vacation, social get-togethers, or assisting the local Narcotics Anonymous planning committee for their annual conference. She was really good at planning something special for the holidays. Christmas was her favorite; though, she could make any special occasion something to remember. She would obsess about executing her plans until she felt assured everything was just right. It could be downright exhausting to watch her in action. But, her objective was to create memories, and the best experience for all who attended these gatherings and events.

Considering her extrovert tendencies, of course, these occasions weren't limited to her children and family. Ma would always invite at least a handful of friends. The drawback to that is, not every invitation, or even confirmed RSVPs, would actually show up. Depending on who the no show was she would be disappointed and/or frustrated, which is pretty normal. Worst case scenario, she might obsess about it for the duration of the occasion. Best case scenario, she could dismiss it. She would say, *"Who's here was supposed to be here."* We ALL felt better in the 'best case scenario' situations. It was no fun watching and hearing her in her feelings about such a matter. Understandably so, since she put so much into her plans for the sake of ensuring a good time for her guests.

Instead I have been driven and determined to create a life that can have an impact on someone else in similar fashion, as she had on me.

However, she learned to cope with those disappointments and decreasingly internalized the no shows. This became another lesson that she would impart to my siblings and me. Now it is a mantra that I repeat to myself to cope in the void of her immediate presence. Operative word is "repeat", because I still very much miss her. I still have moments where I just want her to come back. However, in these years since she passed I have realized more and more the wisdom she had. For me it helps me cope to know she believed "who is supposed to be here, is here".

Again, I would be lying if I said I was always able to cope by applying this mantra to my bereavement. However, when I reflect on how my life has adjusted and shifted in response to losing her I can sometimes see how even in this situation it can be applicable. Even I cannot believe I am saying it. Although, I do believe I would be a much different person were she still here. By different, I mean I would probably be stagnant, comfortable, and naive about the significance of everyday happenings and encounters I have with my loved ones. Instead I have been driven and determined to create a life that can have an impact on someone else in similar fashion, as she had on me. At my wake and body viewing, if there is a slideshow of my life I hope it will awaken a person or several to make the best of the life they are given while they still have a chance to live it. Hence the creation of my business, LIVE In Color Red LLC. Ma completely inspired my business' inception and I am not sure it would have even become a reality otherwise. It is my way of honoring her legacy, which include these mantras and so much more.

I cannot determine the specific time, but at a certain point Ma changed from offering feedback, both when requested and voluntarily, to being more reserved. Instead of speaking on everything on her mind, she would offer a good 'ol "pray about it." Now as much as I previously desired her to keep her unsolicited advice to herself, I would be quite annoyed at this apparent new behavior. How ironic is that?! To this day, I am not sure why she began doing this. Was she humoring me and deciding to give me what I said I wanted all these years? Was she fatigued in helping others problem solve? Had she lost confidence in her own knowledge of life and its challenges? Or perhaps, maybe her own experience in therapy eventually taught her that every question does not require an answer or come with a personal obligation for her to solve? If so, as a therapist I definitely can appreciate her ability to not only learn, but execute that approach.

As a spiritual person, that advice has been a go to in my journey of mourning. Despite my professional knowledge, gaining membership into the Mother loss tribe, sometimes meant that all professional insight was null and void. This was especially true after the funeral and assisting in sorting through Ma's belongings. After all that, the time had come to leave my immediate supports, such as siblings, family friends and Ma's close friends in Southern California, quite a ways from in Atlanta, GA where I reside with my husband and first son at the time.

Talk about loneliness, even despite a strong social support system in Georgia. Actually, I had several moments where I would ask myself… "Where are they?!" I would say to myself, "I just lost my mom and some of you are nowhere to be found!" I believed they had abandoned me in my greatest time of need. It was bad enough to lose my mom and for 'them' to do that to me compounded already complex emotions of bereavement. Needless to say, those thoughts definitely had me in my feelings. But, eventually more rational thoughts replaced them and I was able to embrace understanding on their behalf. For example, it helped to consider the enormity of someone, me in their case, losing a mom. I imagined they didn't want to consider what it's like to lose a mother and have to confront the fact that it will be a reality that most children will have to face one day, or they didn't know what to say because they knew there's nothing that can immediately help take my pain away. Understanding or not, when thinking and speaking from a hurt place, the lack of support I felt I was getting was like being on a call and there being dead silence. I was in pain, but wanted to connect. Thankfully, I was able to determine that 'dead silence' or not, I needed to talk about Ma to someone and found a therapist for my own grief counseling. The additional support was just what I needed for that period of time in my grief process. It is amazing how much difference a listening ear and insight with unconditional regard can make. Yet, that is what my therapist provided me and it helped.

Therapy is great for gaining insight and support, and my experience was no different. In another moment of clarity, I acknowledge that despite being disappointed in others, there were some friends I never used in a supportive capacity, become invaluable support when I needed it. It felt great that they somehow conjured up the courage to be there to give encouragement. To date my favorite responses to my bereavement experience are "that sucks" or "Gail was a great woman I can't imagine what it must be like to lose her". One of the best things for me to do during the sadness and longing periods of my bereavement journey was to take advantage of opportunities to talk about my mom and process my feelings about losing her. Even today, almost five years later, it helps. This would be one of my strongest recommendations to anyone else. Don't be like me and get upset at those who are not emotionally equipped to be that support you need, because there are just as many who are or will. Also, don't hesitate to include a professional, if necessary. It is natural to expect usual supports, such as close friends and family, to provide the proverbial 'shoulder to lean on', except when grief and bereavement is concerned it just is not that straightforward. "Who's here was supposed to be here," can be applied to your support system as well.

By coming to terms with the fact that your mother is no longer with you physically there is an increase likelihood that you can become open to the possibilities of recognizing her love in different presentations and forms. For example, connecting to her love can be found in your pursuit of an experience that you both talked about doing together. It can also be an extension of something that she started that you may want to continue in respect and honor of legacy. Of course, it can be a completely new venture, such as a for-profit or non-profit business. The latter example is perhaps one of the more popular or common platforms chosen by survivors of mothers and loved ones that have passed away.

Utilizing the love for our mothers to find purpose above and beyond what we would have pursued when they were still with us can be (in itself) a linking object to maintain a connection to them. Linking objects are those things that we use to stay connected with loved ones that have died. They typically hold a special meaning for her or your relationship that you want to continue on. Some examples of linking objects may be saving their favorite t-shirt to wear, frame, or be used for a customize project. They can also be a piece of jewelry or furniture, pictures, bible or tattoo. All of the aforementioned differ, but share in common the ability to link us to our love for our mother and the desire to stay connected to her.

One does not have to be accepting of the loss to appreciate the value of a linking object. The countless stories of family members fighting over the possessions of their deceased loved one, can attest to that. In the unfortunate, and hopefully rare occurrence where greed is the driving force, such instances of 'fighting' oftentimes has to do with wanting to have a keepsake of that loved one. Ma loved angels and had several figurines and knick-knacks of all different sorts of angels. Thankfully, there was enough for all of her children to keep at least one angel each as a linking object to her. It's funny how a simple 'object" can have so much value, literally overnight, because it morphs into that 'thing' that maintains a relationship and sort of becomes an inheritance of their energy, as well as, what they represented to the family culture.

I agree with grief and loss expert Alan Wolfelt who encourages in his book, "The Paradoxical Truth of Mourning" that we don't have to rush to rid ourselves of the material possessions when someone dies. We don't even have to immediately change around furniture in their home if we don't want to. Those possessions might be an important link that eventually will promote a healthy adjustment to the loss; otherwise, it runs the risk of being premature and can possibly result in unnecessary regret.

A reflection of when I was in grief, and the mourning process to date, I realize that I've had several linking objects to which I immediately attached to. Although I was still going back and forth between all the different "stages of grief", each linking object had one thing in common; they all assisted me at whatever stage I was in at that time. There was a time when I could not fathom getting rid of anything I kept to remind me of her, yet as I got further and further into healing and adjusting to the new norm I have been able to release myself of certain objects. Over time, some things no longer seemed to hold the same significance and was no longer something I felt was able or necessary to continue to link me to her.

The very nature of bereavement can imitate an adventure in the wilderness. Just as we would prepare for an adventure with supplies and tools for comfort and survival purposes, we have linking objects for our bereavement experience. They allow us to navigate the dynamics of an adventure in mourning. There will be some we only need for a portion of the time (survival) and others that will stay with us for the duration (comfort).

Visitation Dreams, are believed to be dreams that connect us to our mothers after death. They can reveal themselves in the most ethereal way.

The very nature of bereavement can imitate an adventure in the wilderness.

When a visitation dreams occurs, you are 'visited' by the deceased. Not everyone experiences these dreams and not every dream that you have of your mother would be considered a visitation. Not sure if you have experienced a visitation dream? If the following can describe your dream experience with your mother, then perhaps you have. Psychologist and Reiki Master, Anne Reith of Impart Wisdom and Wellness Center, explains that there are 8 characteristics of a Visitation Dream. These characteristics include:

1) A visitation dream feels "real."

2) Visitation dreams are so real and vivid you cannot question if it was real. There might be a natural moment of wonder but in your heart, you will "know".

3) They are very real and vivid dreams so, you WILL remember them.

4) Your mom will appear in the dream healthy in her appearance and in a loving manner. It is rare that they would appear sick or unhealthy. Likewise, their disposition will be positive and never negative. Reith says 'they *will* be "whole, complete, and perfect" because they are now reconnected with "God/Source energy".

5) They will communicate to you very clearly, although it might not be in a verbal capacity.

6) They communicate both verbally and nonverbally, not for small talk, but for a purpose. Once the message is conveyed, they leave.

7) Their messages and presence mostly provide "reassurance" and

support, even if they are giving a warning.

8) You wake up filled with a sense of peace and love.

Are you skeptical or perhaps just curious at how this sort of connection could take place? How can our moms reveal themselves in our dreams?

I believe one would have a great deal of difficulty proving their existence; yet dreams in general are possible because our rational and conscious minds are turned off and the subconscious then has reign to work through things that we likely wouldn't allow them to consciously. Therefore, when the subconscious mind is active without the obstruction of the conscious mind, a visitation dream may be possible and may take place. Of course, you would have to believe in the life after death and spiritual energy to believe any of this.

I believe that I have experienced at least a couple of visitation dreams from my mom. To truly know my mother is to know that she could definitely will her way through the spiritual realm to do it. According to Reith, there is a level of effort required on the parts of the deceased to make the 'visit'. It is a powerful experience! Now that I am more knowledgeable I would definitely define them as visitation dreams. One that I experienced in fact was so strong that I woke up with tears flowing down my cheeks. My mom had visited me and the intensity of the time we shared was almost indescribable. The dream had manifested the sense of void and how much I missed her while I was awake. I remember I was crying out for her and wanted her to know how much I missed her. It was such an intense experience; one I had never experienced before. In other dreams where she was present, it was different. I was more of an observer looking in on some form of an event playing itself out. Truth be told, I like any dream I have of her and I'll take what I can get, but those where she is directly engaged with me and I with her, I cherish the most. Despite the intense emotions that follow the visitation dreams, I ultimately feel comforted by them as yet another reassurance that we are still connected.

I remember I was crying out for her and wanted her to know how much I missed her.

(7)

"Let me put my lips on."

Mourning the death of a loved one is an individual process. There is nothing cookie cutter about it. There are, however, some common techniques that contribute to healthy and sustainable coping. Due to the unique course a person will take to cope and adjust to a loss, there are hundreds to thousands of ways to do so. It just depends on what works for the individual.

With the loss of my mother, there have been three approaches in particular that I have found to be helpful time and time again for me, as well as for clients that I've worked with. The first is spirituality. The benefits of spirituality during challenging times seem to have a positive effect on bereaved persons. Admittedly, for some spirituality has a neutral, at best, effect on their overall adjustment. To clarify, spirituality does not have to mean subscribing to a particular religion or religious practices. It is more so a focus on the beliefs and values systems that promote hope, comfort, and encouragement. Whereas, hyper religiosity can promote or be pushed inappropriately to encourage one to stifle feelings of loss, but when exercised properly and in a healthy manner it can be a beneficial mechanism. In addition, spirituality can serve as a platform for the healing and the understanding that is necessary to facilitate the identification and association with a new norm without your mother. Spirituality plays an integral part in my healing journey. I can definitely say my mom modeled the importance and significance of spirituality in my life. My mom had to overcome many things in her life, including addiction to multiple substances, and her spirituality was something she credited all the time for her ability to overcome those challenges and probably others she never spoke on.

In my private practice I am transparent about my religious beliefs, when asked. Although, it is not something that I force on clients I work with. Yet in my experience those that I have served for grief oriented issues have notated spirituality as a form of resiliency they rely on to cope. A few of the most common spirituality practices include: prayer, meditation, immersing into nature for solitude, and going to a church/synagogue/mosque. In bereavement, at times we may feel inclined to isolate from everyone because the idea and the reality of connecting to others can feel overwhelming or undesirable in an emotionally charged state. Try to avoid that urge. In contrast, it can be beneficial to seek solitude for the purpose of fostering emotional renewal and rejuvenation. Not to mention, simply taking an opportunity to reset so that you can feel better capable of managing the change(s) that are associated to losing a mom.

Social support is another factor with proven benefits to aid in coping. Of course, this is only beneficial when you are surrounded by positive and healthy supports. Maybe those supports are people that are already in your life, such as friends and family, or they are those you form relationships with because of a shared experience in losing a mom. The sweet spot in all that is that they be able to accommodate your emotional needs. In psychology, the impact of social experiences and relationships are believed to play a major role in not only our personal development, but our well-being in general. Therefore it makes sense that one should benefit from utilizing their social support for additional resources and validation in general and for specific needs.

Grief and bereavement can feel very lonely. The right supports can make a difference. Although, ideally, receiving adequate support in bereavement is a shared responsibility of initiating and accepting help as needed.

An available and resourceful support system is beneficial during the time of grief and mourning. It can aid the bereavement process quite a bit when we are under stress in any area of our lives that may lead us to regress in one or more areas of functioning (family, career, social, physical health, etc.). As a therapist, when a client is in distress and at risk of functioning impairment, it is my objective to assess their support system. Doing so can help me gain insight on what the client's likely experience will be in managing the intensity and duration of their distress. Whenever I tell my story about my childhood, what I have gone through, and about my mom, people are surprised. There's this saying, "Thank God, you don't look like what you've been through!" My family is definitely an example and testimony of that, especially my mom. She was beautiful. Not to be superficial or focus on superficial matters, but it is the truth. I would be remiss to not celebrate that given her past. If such is the case for you or your mother, feel free to celebrate that as well. It is something to reflect on as a positive, just as a soldier that has gone to war and come back with little to no injury.

A soldier rarely survives war time without other soldiers alongside them. Similarly, having a tried-and-true support system throughout the trials and tribulation of my mom's life, directly had a positive impact for my siblings and my own life. I am grateful for a mother, chosen by a higher power to birth and raise me, to have this way of staying connected and being resourceful enough to establish a support system (i.e. individuals and community agencies). I would also be remiss if I didn't mention that she did very well in choosing the man that is my biological father - James Bishop. They may not have worked out, but he remained actively engaged throughout my life. At times he and other supports would have to fill in the gap when Mom was in rehab, attending sobriety meetings heavily, and/or working two jobs. These supports were physically present and also supplemented her goals and standards for us.

Ma modeled the significance of a support system, so I can credit that model on how I have been able to manage her death by utilizing my own support system. While I have taken my fair share of opportunities to seek solitude and find ways to process her absence, I'd like to think that I equally have sought out the support from other men and women that, too, have lost their mothers. My own therapist is an example, and to a minor extent, even social media. As someone of the human race (if I might take it there) you have a need to be connected interpersonally. To isolate and withdraw for significant periods is to go against nature and a need for socialization. I'd encourage anyone struggling in their mourning process to determine where you can enlarge your support system and/or lean more on the supports you already have if they have the capacity to accommodate.

One of the greatest contributions to my resiliency since Ma passed can be accounted for by the unexpected, yet awesome support from those that did not happen to be in my 'close' social circle. I believe that by giving myself permission to verbalize how significant my mom's death was for me and

A soldier rarely survives war time without other soldiers alongside them.

the pain I was experiencing, in turn, others felt open to support me in ways they may not have prior to losing my mom. It is ironic that those whom I expected to be there would actually minimize their encounters with me or became absent altogether, while those that I would not have expected were there. I guess that is how the grief cookie crumbles. Right?! Right. Who doesn't like cookies, anyway?

My process of bereavement, including the inspiration from my mother, has shown this to be the case. Indeed, the process probably does not look like anything you can imagine, so be mindful of the expectations you have. Instead, feel free to feel right at home in comfort of the support that is available to you.

Ma was known and loved for a lot of things. Whether by physical or interpersonal standards, she was special and unique. In addition to her resourcefulness and ability to make something out of nothing time and time again, she also had this unique and contagious laugh that could be picked out from anywhere. In truth, when I was younger I would get kind of embarrassed by how loud and high pitch it was. Still, even I couldn't deny its allure. Once she started and kept going, eventually anyone around would find themselves laughing as well. She loved to laugh and did so often. I now see how special that made her. It amazing how different we can view things when we choose to look through them with different lenses. For example, one of her more subtle ways of self-care that I honestly could not fully appreciate in the past, was her obsession with red lipstick. When I tell you, my sisters and I would cringe sometimes because red lips didn't always seem to 'fit' the occasion. But, Ma and her red lipstick was for all intents and purposes non-negotiable. Regardless of any commentary encouraging her against wearing it she'd comeback with, "let me put my lips on", and she would grab her bright and vibrant red lipstick. Allow me to age myself for a moment... If you are familiar with the brand, my mom probably kept Fashion Fair Cosmetics in business from all the red lipstick she purchased. Okay,

It is amazing how different we can view things when we choose to look through them with different lenses.

not really, but seriously her red lips was her signature look, she wore it no matter the season, or what color she was wearing- it was her thing. I believe it illustrated her vibrant personality and that no matter what she was going through or how out of control she felt she had her red lipstick and style to help make herself feel better. I imagine it could have been her way of staying grounded. Life was often stressful for her, so when she would pull out that red lipstick and put it on, she could just be present in that moment with being beautiful and bold. Likewise, in times of stress, sadness, and/or anxiety, we need something that keeps us grounded something that returns us to a sense of safety.

In therapy, "grounding" is a common technique to bring our emotions back into balance when we feel overwhelmed by our memories or current circumstances. They are very beneficial and aid in promoting the therapeutic and healing process. Just like water, it is human nature to avoid too much discomfort and things that are fear evoking; go the path of resistance if you will. We can feel discomfort and fearful in life and in therapy until we are able to resolve stress triggers. Hence, the need to ground ourselves and being active in our self-care is a good way to do that. Most importantly, by staying intentional in practicing self-care, including grounding exercises, we limit maladaptive behaviors that keep us in an avoidant state and on the run from our own feelings and reality. Whereas avoidance and fleeing from difficult emotions can be beneficial in extreme distress, whenever possible, try not to. It's important not to make your conditions much harder or to further complicate physical and emotional symptoms.

Self-care is as it implies; an action or activity that involves taking care of self. During that activity the focus is on what feels good to you for the purpose of destressing and renewing yourself physically, emotionally, mentally, spiritually, or all of the above. In my experience, many people have difficulty practicing this because of fear of being, "selfish". I'll have to admit, I am guilty of perceiving others as selfish instead of self caring, including my mom, when I did not know better. Now I know that's the furthest thing from the truth. If you struggle with allowing yourself sufficient self-care, then consider it as something similar to a bank account. How many deposits you put in to your account is how many withdrawals and purchases you can make. If you make too many withdrawals or purchases in the excess of the amount of the deposits into the 'bank' you will become negligent and overdraft from the account. Eventually, you will be unable to continue to make withdrawals or purchases.

Similarly when we give of ourselves to family, friends, our jobs, community organizations, school, home, and more - we can deplete our physical, emotional, spiritual, and mental "bank accounts". Inadequate and inconsistent self-care replenishment in the face of losing a mother can

Inadequate and inconsistent self-care replenishment in the face of losing a mother can put our well-being 'accounts' in deficit very rapidly.

put our well-being 'accounts' in deficit very rapidly. In this case self-care is necessary. I can pinpoint three ways my mom modeled self-care consistently and unapologetically. Ironically, the memories of her executing self-care has been helpful in my mourning journey. Though, of course they can also be a trigger of longing for her presence. It sounds like quite a Catch 22, and it is. Though, as explained in the book *'The Paradoxes of Mourning"* as written by Alan Wolfelt, the more I have said 'hello' in the midst of saying 'goodbye' to my mom the more present it feels she is here with me.

One of my earliest memories is of my family traveling from Jacksonville, Florida to San Diego, California because we were relocating for a new military assignment my dad had to report to. I guess being married to a man in the Navy for ten years can make a person comfortable with moving around and traveling. My mom was no different. We frequently traveled as a family. Ma would frequently travel by herself with friends. I learned that this was Ma's way of prioritizing her self-care.

Travel during bereavement has proven to be a healthy dose of healing and "reset" for me. I loved to travel before losing my mother, but being in a different environment to mourn away from the day to day hustle and responsibilities seems to facilitate much needed self-care that could be difficult otherwise. Not to mention, travel promotes an easy going attitude to just be present with where you are, without any pressure or negative influences, but a focus to mending your broken heart. Of course, in its most simplistic purpose, travel allows a person to escape their reality. Whereas, that might not reap any long-term benefit, the temporary benefits justifies the experience, so take a trip if you can.

Speaking of benefits, it would be a crime to identify types of self-care that is helpful for coping, without mentioning music. The fondest memories I have of my childhood include music because my mom loved to listen and dance to it. I believe I have long since learned to use music as a tool for coping due to the model set by her. Music can comfort and conjure up memories. It can reflect our current mood and facilitate a mood we would rather have. It can be a voice to our feelings when the words escape us. It can be a distraction to feelings we have difficulty detaching from. Music can stand the test of time. It has an ability to reach us at every level of consciousness. That in itself validates its power.

Music has been a must have on my own journey in adjusting and mourning. Having a playlist or keeping a mental note of specific songs to play during especially emotional times is an example of how to use music to cope. In my experience, it was particularly helpful for me to listen to songs that had a slow to medium tempo that prompted me to be calm and/or reminded me of times of simplicity, laughter, fun, and when my mom was in good health. Artists and groups such as Sade, Kenny G, BeBe & CeCe Winans, Sounds of Blackness, Hall and Oates, Patti Labelle, Gap band, etc. are on the short list of what my mom would play over and over again. Therefore, they serve as my go-to's when I have a grief burst or long to be in her presence through my memories of her.

The funny thing is, Ma could not sing, like at all, but that did not stop her. Similarly, nothing would stop her from dancing if one of her songs came on, regardless of who was around. It is that spirit that I have grown to love to seek out, although she is absent from me physically. The memories of her are the best comfort I have readily available to me. I am thankful that I haven't been separated from those memories in any way yet. She still remains in my thoughts and heart. She will forevermore until we meet again.

Bonus Narratives: Let's Turn Together

Mommy magic is real. It is why losing a mother can be so difficult. But consider this, mom's magic does not die with the absence of her physical presence. It may take some time recognizing, because it has a different appearance. Also, it may be hard to accept it in its changed form. However, it is there if we open ourselves to it. Not convinced? The following stories from the children of mothers that have transitioned, at various ages and stages of their lifespan, provide touching and inspiring narratives about how mommy magic can transcend death.

Meet Earl

30-something holistic health coach. New York native. Lives in California. Music enthusiast.

"Choose the Sweet Life"

Her name was Margaret Washington. I was thirty-four when she passed and she was seventy-four. There were some circulation complications that started with her heart valve replacement some years back. What originally got her to that point was a surgery to tie the vein off in one of her ankles. It never took like it was expected to, having continued circulation issues and winding up having heart valve replacement. One day she complained of extreme burning in her lower extremities and her feet. This was in March 2012 and I happened to be visiting in town that day. Her burning continued into the next day. My dad said let's take her to the hospital. She was sent back home with a diagnosis of sciatic nerve tissue. I thought that was a little weird. As a trainer, most of my clients didn't experience sciatic pain so far in life.

Mom's pain never really subsided. My father took her back to the hospital, the pain worsened and her leg started to turn colors. They brought her back to the hospital, and while she was there they performed several tests to no avail. After all the back and forth, it turned out she had a blood clot and wound up amputating one of her legs. They did what they could in that moment and several months passed before they took the other leg.

It was hard to watch this happen to my mom because I think oxygen deprivation and medications had to do with the dementia she was experiencing. We went back and forth with that for a few years. In 2015, the leg started worsening to the point where she had to have hospice care because gang green started to set in. It was really nothing we could do, and that's how it happened.

Prior to 2012 my mom's health was good. She was probably one of the biggest proponents to me going into the field of health and fitness. She was very conscious about what she ate and she would often test out some new fitness DVD or equipment. It is because of her that I am the trainer I am today.

Initially, I felt an overwhelming obligation to my father to try my best to smoothen his journey. He and my mom had been married for 56 years. She was nineteen and he was twenty-one when they married. My love for him, is why I just jumped into action. It may have been my way of coping, I don't know. I didn't give myself too much time to let it sink in and process, because I just wanted to look out for him. It was weird. I did have to distinguish the two different relationships. I lost my mama and he lost his wife that he had known since she was a girl. I tried to find the balance. I could not get so caught up in me that I did not consider others.

The most challenging part for me was not feeling some kind of way with people who did not do what was expected of them, were not present, or had disappointing behavior when petitions were made. I try to remember, people are people and they deal how they deal, but there are some hurt feelings. I felt a sense of disappointment on my mama's behalf. We had a good relationship. I'm at peace. I have resolve. I honestly believe she didn't go on. She fought hard, but her faith remained in God. I think I made her proud prior to passing. My pursuit in life is to honor her. There's nothing in life I take for granted now, like for real for real. When it was all said and done, I was so thankful. I put my mind on being thankful. The best thing you can do is dwell on thinking about how and what are you supposed to get from life. Having witnessed my mom, I was blessed to see how you are supposed to die. I know it sounds crazy, but I was able to see her on her journey be so ironclad, faithful, full of resolve, and peace. When they told her she was going to lose her leg she started saying, 'thank you Jesus, that I had 70 something years with these legs'.

When I walk, I do it for my mama. Everything you are blessed to go through it can help someone else.

Earl's tip to the tribe: Look for strength in the memories of your loved ones and don't be afraid to feel. In allowing yourself to feel, that's where healing takes place.

Meet Kim

30-something Licensed Clinical Social Worker. Florida raised.
Lives in North Carolina. Dedicated Mom.

"Mom, can you come say something to me please!"

My mom's name was Olivia Bailey Simmons and she had a long history of health problems, dating back to 1999 when she had a major stroke. She was not expected to make it through the night, but she was a fighter and she fought her way to defy the odds. "She won't walk," they said. Yes, she did. "She won't talk," they said. Yes, she did. "She won't drive," they said. Yes she did. "She won't live independently," they said. Yes, she did. She did not accept "no," "won't," or "can't." Years later, my mother was diagnosed with renal kidney failure, which required frequent dialysis, while awaiting a kidney transplant. She was blessed to receive a transplant on August 24, 2010.

In late 2013 and into 2014, she started not feeling too well, but she didn't really tell us or at least I don't remember those details. Leading up to the summer of 2014, I had made the decision to move to Greensboro, North Carolina, where she and one of my sisters lived with her family. At this time, my daughter was 14 months old and I wanted her to be closer to my mom. I remember her feeling a lack of enthusiasm about us coming. She wasn't as excited as I anticipated her being, but when I asked, she just said that she was not feeling well. She had been diagnosed with Pancreatitis, and despite pain medications and many doctor visits, there was no relief for her. She began to experience a frustrating cycle - hospital, to rehab, to being back at home, then back in the hospital...a number of times.

I remember one day we were at one hospital going over the results for her colonoscopy with the doctor and she asked, "do I have cancer?!" I was surprised by that because we don't have a strong family history of cancer. The doctor said no, and I was relieved. We continued the cycle, and one day when she was home with a friend, she called me at work to tell me that she was going to the hospital. I was on the phone and overhear the paramedics coming in. She told them that she wanted to go to a hospital across the county line, where she received her kidney transplant. A place that she trusted. They did scans, and immediately saw the tumor. In early October, a biopsy was completed, which confirmed that the tumor was cancerous. She died the next month on the morning of November 17, 2014 from Pancreatic Cancer. I was thirty-five.

My mother and I were very, very close. I came to North Carolina because I needed help; to be close to immediate family as a single parent. When we arrived on June 28th, my mom was in the hospital and passed within five months. It was a Monday, and it just so happened that I had already taken the day off of work to handle some business as the Power of Attorney for her. The previous Friday, the hospice nurse visited and told me that she felt that my mother would pass "any day now." At this point, I was sleeping in the same room as her since she was in a hospital bed. I woke up and said good morning, touched her and went to go take a shower. I could see that she was breathing. Her cousin was visiting, so she went to speak to my mother as I left the room. I came out of the shower, went back into the room, and I could immediately feel that something had changed. I called out to her and stared at her chest for a moment, hoping to see movement. Due to dialysis, my mother had a fistula in her upper right arm, which was always raised and firm. I walked to her, and when I touched her right arm, I felt that it was flat and soft.

I called hospice and the nurse and social worker on duty were the ones originally assigned to my mother's case. They arrived quickly and the nurse recorded the time of death. My dad was the first one to answer the phone as I called with the news. Once I heard his voice, all I could do was wail, and say, "she's gone!"

It was weird. I don't know where my mind went. I was outside taking pictures of my daughter, when a lady who assisted with caring for my mom while I worked, walked up stopping by for a visit. I told her, "Oh I'm so sorry. She just passed." I don't know what kind of fight or flight I was in but I remember not really being all there. I look back on that time and I don't think I've had a real break down yet. I think it's because I feel like I can't. I don't want sad energy around my daughter.

I wonder if I am mad at her for dying. I don't know, maybe. She was always a fighter - through her stroke, her kidney failure, and anything else that came her way. She couldn't fight the cancer and I did not understand that. I've been tense for three years. Anxiety is a battle. I don't feel like she has visited me and that has bothered me. I'm like why not?! Mom, can you come say something to me please! I do recall one time when I was putting my daughter to bed. She was staring at me and began to rub the back of her finger softly, up and down on my cheek. That was a gesture my mom would always do to me and on that one occasion, I felt that she was speaking through my daughter.

When I have emotional moments, I am by myself. I am a private griever, or maybe I just don't know what to say. It's interesting; being a mom without having a mom to tell me how to be a mom. I feel she would tell me the right answers, but I can't ask her. I do try to look at what has happened and what God is trying to teach me. I do think that part of my lesson in this is to let people help me, as I have constantly been the helper. My mom was always the helper, as well.

With my anxiety and sadness, I worry that I am not making her proud. It is very important to me to be mindful of living in a way that she would be proud of. I also think of ways to honor my mother and make sure my daughter knows her. For instance, getting the city's proclamation for Pancreatic Cancer Awareness Month. For her birthday this year, my sisters and I, along with our children, each released three balloons, representing the number of her birthdays that we have been without her. Their spirits stay alive as long as we continue to speak their names!

In a letter that my mother wrote to the family of her kidney donor, she said, "My life has been a journey that has travelled many peaks and valleys. In all of it, I know that God was by my side, and many times carried me. The last decade has had many physical challenges that gave me several lessons - one about patience; another, appreciation; and most of all, about faith." These three things can help us through this most difficult time. Be patient with yourself and your individual grieving process. Be appreciative of the times that you had with your mother and think back on them often, with a smile. Have faith to know that you will make it.

Kim's tip to the tribe: Remember to care for yourself. The days and months after the funeral service can be harder than the initial impact. Allow yourself to feel and grieve as needed.

Meet Fawna

30-something HR professional. Native of Detroit, MI. Lives in Los Angeles area. Loves to laugh.

"You don't really talk about this kind of mother loss. It's just a smaller percentage of people that can relate."

Her name was Phyllis Jean Banks and she died on February 11, 2001. I was 20 years old and a junior in college. We all thought it was fate that I drove up to Detroit in my car a week before she died and I saw her for a couple of days. Then I drove back. She died on the following Sunday and I didn't find out until Monday. I got a knock on the door from the Tallahassee police telling me that I needed to go to the counseling center at school. I really didn't think anything, but I walked over there. I didn't think it was a family death at all, just that it was random to me. I get there and remember sitting in front of this lady in her office. She told me, "they found your mother dead", and there was shock. Of course, I just cried. I cried off and on the rest of the day. I called a cousin of mine to tell him the news and he told me, "My dad told me he got Steve to turn himself in." I was like, "what are you talking about?" and he was like, "oh you didn't know? Steve did it."

I turned on the news and basically found out that my stepdad had come home after being away being away for about a month or so, got into an argument and subsequently stabbed my mom. She wanted a divorce. He said he thought that killing her was the best thing for their kids. It was surreal. We became "that family", "that situation", that was on the news. His family came over and took everything and left us with nothing.

The funeral day was okay, and I cried. He took her life and that was just hard. I tried to see him in jail, I mean I didn't hate him, but I wanted answers, like why? Why did he do it? The next time I saw him was in court, years later. It was a two week trial, I was there for one week. He was convicted for 2nd degree murder. His sentence was 20 or 40 years with a chance of parole. They couldn't prove it was premeditated. It probably hit me weeks or months later and I have moments where I cry to myself.

You don't really talk about this kind of mother loss. It's just a smaller percentage of people that can relate. It's a little bit different, but it's still the same. When you get married your mother won't be there. My mom will never see my kids. You think about those things and it just SUCKS! I don't think I've dealt with it. It's been packed away. When it happened I was focused on getting back to school. I think getting back and finishing school was something my mom would be proud of. That was pretty much it, because I remember her saying to me, "I'm just so proud you're in school." That was kind of the last thing she said to me. I had to finish.

I haven't had therapy to help me deal with it. As for my

stepfather, I don't hate him, but he's out of sight so out of mind. I could never have a relationship with him. My humor reminds me of her humor. I made a scrapbook of different things of hers and I will go through it from time to time. Right now life is a little tough, I wish I could talk to my mom and ask for advice. You start to get used to it. When it comes to sharing what happened sometimes you just don't want to hear a reaction. I don't need that extra. I have had to be independent. That is one thing that has come from this.

Fawna's tip to the tribe: Learn to forgive and not let anger or bitterness eat you up. Find peace whether it takes months or years.

Meet Angela

50 something Licensed Therapist. Chicago native. Lives in Atlanta. Enjoys running 5k races.

"I get this life thing now. I'm going to keep living and people are going to keep going."

I think it was just her heart that gave out. My initial reaction was very sad, but I still think about the manner in which it happened. It was such a peaceful sort of quiet transition that made it easier to deal with. The nurse for my mom took really good care of her. She told me that just two days prior to her death, that she said, "I'm ready." So, I think she was at peace. The toughest day that I had in relation to this whole thing was my birthday; my first birthday without her. Every time I say that, I get teary eyed. It's just really tough when you realize that you do not have a parent to say 'Happy Birthday' to you. It's just like WOW; nobody that gave me birth is here. It's really mind boggling that this is how it ends up! Angela at 55 years old says, "I get this life thing now. I'm going to keep living and people are going to keep going. This is how the circle of life flows. A parent is a different type of loss."

Her mother, Eunice Elizabeth Jones Hardiman passed in 2015 at age 92. Angela's father died when she was in college. Angela speaks of being initially shocked when she arrived and was able to view her mother firsthand. Yet, Angela has a sense of acceptance and is at peace with her mother transitioning and says for the better part of her bereavement she has felt this way. She accounts this to her mother's age and long life, Eunice's belief in Jesus Christ that would allow her to spend the afterlife in Heaven, and the peace of saying and showing her love for her mother while she was alive. Eunice's death has motivated Angela to take every opportunity to travel and enjoy life while she can. During an international trip to the country Ghana, Angela woke up at sunrise and spread a portion of her mother's ashes in the Atlantic Ocean. In totality, her mother's ashes went into Lake Michigan, some in the Mississippi River, and around her sister's grave. Angela put it simply. "What if I don't get to live until I'm 92? I need to enjoy things now."

Angela's Tip: Grief is so individualized. Don't let others make the assumption that your pain is any less if you are okay that your mother is at peace. Also, work to remain comfortable with where your relationships are, with those you care about.

Meet Linda

30-something Social Worker. Lives in Washington DC.

"I coped with loss in other ways."

Linda is thirty years old now, but she lost her mother at the age of eighteen. Her mother, Patricia G., was diabetic and died at age 51 from complications of the condition, seemingly unexpectedly. This put Linda in a state of shock that led to her avoidance of losing her mom for at least a decade following her passing. Linda says "I coped with my loss in other ways. Looking for love in men who did not care about me and I stayed extremely busy. "

Though, her journey toward healing and mending her broken heart from the loss of Patricia was delayed, she has been able to work through her grief and mourn in a fashion that is leading her to a "God...greater purpose" such as helping other women that are also a part of the mother loss tribe.

In part, she mentions that her lack of emotional support or someone to talk to, impacted her ability to mourn her mother at first.

However, now she has several insights. She hopes her story of loss will encourage others that have lost their mothers.

Linda's tip for the tribe: I would say remember the good times and process the not so good times. Love yourself, remember it is okay to cry, and take it one day at a time.

Meet Zdany

30-something Saxophone Recording Artist. Tampa native. Lives in Atlanta. Loves DIY projects.

"Only What You Do For Christ Will Last."

Mama was Maxine Thomas Chisholm and she was sixty years old when she passed. I was just eighteen. My initial reaction was a fluster of emotions. I was of course heartbroken to the thought of losing my first true love, my best friend, my everything; but on the other hand, a little relieved that she would not have to suffer anymore from the pains, ups and downs, struggles, emotional rollercoaster and especially the chemo… All of that was over. During most of her battle, I was away in college. I didn't really get to see all of the immediate day to day struggles, pains, trips to the doctor for chemo, hair falling out, and other emotions that my father and brother experienced. I was made aware of everything along the way, but being the baby of the family, I think they tried to protect me from the bulk of it so that I could focus on school. I was in my sophomore year at Florida A&M University when the phone call from my brother was received. It was on a Sunday. I'll never forget. He simply said, "You need to get home (Tampa). They don't think mom will make it through the night." I immediately put some things in a bag and rushed home.

The drive from Tallahassee usually takes about four hours. I did it in just about three. To this day, I'm thankful for traveling grace, mercy, and for getting me there safely. When I arrived to the hospital to meet family, I entered the room to see my mom in the bed. They announced that I was there and she smiled. Truly caught up in emotions, I vaguely recall anything after that moment other than just sitting with her and spending time. Sometime went by and I remember leaving the room a bit emotional, as I went down the hall to a vending machine. As I was walking back down the hall to the room, I could tell that something had changed with all of the different emotions going on from family. My mama had just passed moments after I left the room. It was evident that she was holding on just for her baby boy, but she didn't want me to be there when she took her last breath.

Early on the most challenging part was just dealing with the fact that I would not be able to pick up the phone, talk to my mama, or even see her again. She is dearly missed and loved, but I know that she's in a much better place. I'm sure she is proud of her sons. My mom in particular had a couple sayings that she would always say to us, "Only What You Do for Christ Will Last" and "Always Establish Your Own Identity!" Those two sayings have mainly been the pillars in my life. The latter has been my driving force with everything that I do. I even got "Own Identity" tattooed on my arm to never forget that being yourself is most important. It's okay to admire, and/or study others, but always be the best version of yourself that you can be.

Zdany's tip to the tribe: Your loved one will always be in your heart, so honor them by living your best life while maintaining the core lessons, morals, and values that they tried to instill.

Meet Gloria

50-something government employee. New York native. Lives outside Atlanta. The life of the party.

"Every year I go back to the cemetery to visit."

My mom's name was Louise Void. She was born on August 10, 1921 and she passed on July 8, 2009 from what they said was stomach cancer, but they didn't really know because it had already spread through her body. When I was younger we didn't get along, but as we got older we got closer. We were truly alike in many ways. She would cook for me. My food would be sitting there waiting for me when I came home from work. After she retired, she kept all the grandkids and some great grandkids, but you had to pay her. All the kids drank coffee and everyone loved her. She said what she meant and didn't care whose feelings were hurt.

We found out mom was sick, I became her caregiver. I went to the doctor, did her banking; I did everything. I kept my siblings in the loop and it was an everyday thing that I was at her house. At a certain point they told us she had six months to live. She had a hospice nurse who was really good. The hospice nurse told us that we needed to call our family because the time was near. She didn't want to die in a hospital, so we brought her home. Everybody said their goodbyes. I was the last to talk to her and I said, "I'm going to be okay." She kind of closed her eyes and passed after that. I'm one of those strong people who doesn't really cry. At the funeral I was good, but then I couldn't breathe and I had to get up and leave. After that I was okay. That was on a Monday and I moved out of New York on that Friday.

Every year I go back to the cemetery to visit. That's how close we were. The first couple of years it was bad, but I've gotten better at dealing with the grief. At first, I just went back to business as usual. Now lately I just want to live. My way of grieving is in celebrating life now. I have lost a mother, a father, and a sibling and each one affected me differently, but my mom affected me the most. It isn't something that one can be truly prepared for. I'm going to a therapist now because I started feeling like something was wrong with me. I have learned that I was a little depressed and it probably started when my mom passed. I am learning how to be open about things and talk about them, which is not something I do well. One thing I cannot do is attend the funeral service for someone's parent yet. I still have my moments. I don't try to hide it. I just cry and I do so because you have to; you just have to let it go. I may not talk about it to anybody but I do a lot of crying.

Gloria's tip to tribe: If you still have time to spend with your mother, do so. It's something you cannot get from anyone else. If she is already gone, remember ALL the times you enjoyed together.

Meet Shamika

A 30-something state employee and student. Atlanta born and raised. Friendly, creative, and mature beyond her years.

"I hated not having that family, or what I thought should be a normal life for a child."

I remember her getting sick. My mother and I were very close. She was a stay at home mom, so we spent a lot of time together. She was also a really good mom. My brother and I went to a private school and the pastor's family of the church of the school took us in. Once mom started getting real bad off, I guess she didn't want us to see her like that. I remember them packing our stuff up saying we were going to see our mom. I was so excited. When we got home, she was gone. She was literally gone. I thought she was hiding, but she wasn't. I asked my dad, "where is mom?!" He told us she had passed away.

It was 1986. I was six. I was devastated by her death. I dealt a lot with it by reading. I would isolate myself and I would read. Being without my mother was the hardest. It's just like when I got my period I didn't have anyone to tell me about that. We didn't have internet like that, so I learned by hearing other girls say this is what happened and this is what my mom did.

I would also write. I wrote poems and stories to get through it, but things were hard. I had a lot of days in which I cried. I hated not having that family, or what I thought should be a normal life for a child. As a child, I said I didn't want any kids. I didn't want to leave them alone like my mom left me.

When I found out I was pregnant I was devastated. I got pregnant because I got raped by a guy I was dating. Once I became a mother, I decided I would deal with it. I definitely went to therapy. Even though she wasn't here physically, I always felt like mom was my guardian angel. I have been through some tough situations and I came out unharmed. I always feel it's because my guardian angel has helped me. I still talk to her. It doesn't beat her being here, but there's nothing I can do about that.

Shamika's note to the tribe: I really can't offer advice on how to deal with the grief you experience from losing a mother because that is a tremendous loss for any person at any age and everyone grieves differently. Even though I was only a young child, I remember that my mom loved GOD. She taught me to always pray and love GOD too and so I did. I prayed and I developed a relationship with GOD at a young age. That relationship got me through the grief and the sorrow. That's what kept me going and never let me give up.

Note to Readers:

Dealing with grief and loss is not easy. On top of that, it can oftentimes feel very lonely. Without knowing your story of loss, I know something about it prompted you to read this book. I am honored and humbly extend my sincere thanks and gratitude for the opportunity to offer my experience and some guidance. I can only hope to have helped ease the sting of your loss, if even just a little bit. While your journey most definitely will not stop here, I pray your path will ultimately be that of comfort and peace.

Author Denesha Chambers

Author's Bio

Denesha Chambers has been a Licensed Therapist for almost 10 years, and has recently become a Certified Grief Specialist. In 2013, she founded L.I.V.E. In Color Red LLC, a business whose name was inspired by her mom's love for the color and drive to turn losses in life into valuable lessons. On the very, very, very short list faith, family, the beach, her work through LICR, music, and chocolate bring her joy.

Bibliography

1. Stage of grief models: Kubler-Ross http://www.amhc.org/58-grief-bereavement-issues/article/8444-stage-of-grief-models-kubler-ross

2. Narrative Therapy Centre

http://www.narrativetherapycentre.com/narrative.html

3. Feeling wheel

http://blogs.edweek.org/teachers/coaching_teachers/Feeling-Wheel.jpg

4. Grief.com

5. Vicarious bereavement (grief)

http://www.deathreference.com/A-Bi/Bereavement-Vicarious.html

6. Visitation dreams https://www.annereith.com/8-characteristics-of-visitation-dreams/

7. Anticipatory Grief

https://whatsyourgrief.com/anticipatory-grief/

8. *The Paradoxes of Mourning: Healing your grief with three forgotten truths.* Wolfelt, Alan; July 2015.

Made in the USA
Lexington, KY
09 November 2019